Young
2004 POETRY

ONCE UPON A RHYME

IMAGINATION FOR A NEW GENERATION

. . . Poetically Ever After

Edited by Claire Tupholme

 Young**Writers**

First published in Great Britain in 2004 by:
Young Writers
Remus House
Coltsfoot Drive
Peterborough
PE2 9JX
Telephone: 01733 890066
Website: www.youngwriters.co.uk

SB ISBN 1 84460 572 8

Foreword

Young Writers was established in 1991 and has been passionately devoted to the promotion of reading and writing in children and young adults ever since. The quest continues today. Young Writers remains as committed to engendering the fostering of burgeoning poetic and literary talent as ever.

This year's Young Writers competition has proven as vibrant and dynamic as ever and we are delighted to present a showcase of the best poetry from across the UK. Each poem has been carefully selected from a wealth of *Once Upon A Rhyme* entries before ultimately being published in this, our twelfth primary school poetry series.

Once again, we have been supremely impressed by the overall high quality of the entries we have received. The imagination, energy and creativity which has gone into each young writer's entry made choosing the best poems a challenging and often difficult but ultimately hugely rewarding task - the general high standard of the work submitted amply vindicating this opportunity to bring their poetry to a larger appreciative audience.

We sincerely hope you are pleased with our final selection and that you will enjoy *Once Upon A Rhyme . . . Poetically Ever After* for many years to come.

Contents

William Priest (10)	20
George Campbell (8)	21
Thomas Lowde (8)	22
Olivia Schofield (9)	22
Izzy Arkwright (8)	23
Sophia Colville (9)	23
Charlie Newman (9)	24
Isabella Boscawen (9)	24
Freddie Waller (8)	24
Lydia Newman Saville (9)	25
Christian James (8)	25
Jock Jamieson-Black (8)	25
Georgia Miles (9)	26
Jonathan Berry (8)	26
George Jackson (8)	27
Florence Grellier (9)	28
Hector Campbell (9)	28
Anna Lamport (11)	29
Ben Field (8)	29
Bertie Scott-Hopkins (7)	30
Charles Carden (7)	30
Clementine Melvin (7)	31
Luke Henry (8)	31
Jamie Penmore (7)	32
Rowland Graham (7)	32
Emily Knight (7)	32
Jessica Priest (7)	33
Michael Young (8)	33
Ellie Bleeker (7)	33
Isabel Tanner (10)	34
Alexandra Wharton (10)	34
Rosie Gordon Lennox (11)	35
Will Purcell (10)	35
Lydia Rogers (10)	36
Camilla Weston (9)	36
Roanna Castle (10)	37
Sebastian Clarke (10)	37
Emily Verschoyle (7)	38
James Boggis-Rolfe (9)	38
George Hunt (10)	39
Jack Dalrymple Hamilton (9)	39
Tom Stafford-Michael (9)	40

Celia Garland (10)   64
Lauren Underwood (11)   65

Christ Church CE Primary School, Coseley

Shellie Noakes (9)   65
Danielle Thomas (10)   66
Steven Powell (10)   66
Gavin Kelleher (9)   67
Matthew Ball (11)   67
Elli Share (11)   68
Michelle Stevens (10)   69
Stacey Downs (11)   70
Georgina Groom (11)   71
Gemma Davies (10)   72
Stephanie Steventon (11)   73
April Dale (9)   74
Pollyanna Scriven (11)   74
Georgia Walker (11)   75
Chelsea Davies (10)   75
Elliot Rollason (9)   76

Ely Presbyterian Church School, Cardiff

Lynsey Gronow (10)   76
Timothy Solman (10)   77
Alice Lock (6)   77
Matthew Lock (8)   78

Foxmoor School, Stroud

Charlotte Cowley (8)   78
Jared Old (10)   79
Samuel Hawkins (9)   79
Candice Francis (10)   80
Alice Samways (9)   80
Sophie Miller (10)   81
Sam Coates (8)   81
Ben Holden (7)   82
Aurora Bragg (9)   82
Devon Shirley (9)   82
Kane Shill (9)   83
Ellishia Francis (9)   83

Holly Martin (9)	83
Shifra Kirby (8)	84
Charis Wyatt (8)	84
Joshua Ireland (11)	84
Carys Neale (8)	85

Glandwr Primary School, Whitland

Billy Gray (10)	85
Meg Spiers (10)	85
Lukas Grafton (10)	86
Max Grafton (8)	86
Rosy Stark (10)	87
Morgan Halle (9)	87
Zoey Akroyd (11)	88
Murali Painter (11)	89
Ben Akroyd (9)	90
David Pyart (10)	90
Gwynneth Evans (10)	91
Jamie Gray (8)	91

Hob Green Primary School, Stourbridge

Daniel Watkinson (10)	92
Stephanie Lucas (11)	92
Hattie Weaver (8)	92
Kirsty Dea (8)	93
Charlotte McNaughton (11)	93
Jamie Gilliam (6)	93
Saif Ali (9)	94
Emily Flockton (10)	94
Jodie Bostock (8)	95
Matthew Grazier (9)	95
Chelsea Stringer (9)	96
Kyle Hadley (10)	96
Shelby McGann (9)	97
Kieren Kendrick (8)	97
Paige Massey (8)	98
Daniel Gilliam (10)	98
Amy Cox (8)	98
Leighton Soley (9)	99
Connor Rose (8)	99
Daniel Pemberton (7)	99

Charlotte Bond (8)   100
Carla Evans (9)   100
Kirsty Parker (9)   101
Charlotte Portman (9)   101
Luke Jeffries (9)   101
Christopher Watkinson (9)   102
Jodie Doran (8)   102
Alice Skelding (10)   103
Luke Watkinson (10)   103
Kurtis Russell (8)   104
Sophie Lewis (9)   104
Jordan Tanner (10)   105
Hussna Tariq (9)   105
Charlie Lingard (8)   106
Laura Edwards (9)   106
Sophie Radford (10)   107
Jessica Rogers (9)   107
Salman Sadiq (10)   108
Hannah Horton (9)   108
Stacey Jones (9)   109

Lindens Primary School, Sutton Coldfield

Jozef Doyle & George Martin Acton (10)   109
Alex Dudley & Mitchell Ball (9)   110
Robyn Gough & Lakeisha Sewell (10)   110
Rachel Huckfield (9)   110
Elena Tallis, Heidi McManus (10) & Katie Perkins (9)   111
Megan Saul (10) & Josh Finegan (9)   111
Ben Whatley & Arjan Mangat (9)   111
Samuel James Crawford (10) & Oliver Willis (9)   112
Katie Fletcher & Emily Freegard (9)   112
Jade Morris (9)   112
Paul Weston (10)   113
Nicole Flavell-Avery (9)   113
Toni Stevens (10)   113
Joe Geens (9) & Thomas Strawford (10)   114
Alison Black & Sophie Fisher (9)   114

Manorbier VCP School, Tenby

Loren Sawyer (8)   114
Kate Harries (8)   115

Sally Harvey (9)   115
Rowan Griffiths (8)   116
Tom Grover (9)   116
Seth Harvey (7)   116
Jack Wilkinson-Dix (8)   117
Ruby Goddard (8)   117
Chloe Moss (7)   117
Greg William John   118
Scott Bevan (8)   118
Alexandra Holmes (8)   118
Caitlin Buck (7)   119
Logan Cardy (8)   119
Milea Williams (9)   119
Emma Grimbaldeston (10)   120
Aniya Louise Thornton (10)   120
Jonathon Morris (8)   120
Rebecca Williams (10)   121
Chloe Lewis (7)   121
Holly Walker (8)   121
Lloyd Davies (10)   122
Roxanne Walker (11)   122
Sarah Giffard (11)   123
George Scott (10)   123
Sophie Wilson (10)   124
Abi Markham (11)   124
Jack Grover (10)   124
Josh Noott (9)   125
Aimee May Lewis (9)   125
Charley Aspley (8)   125
Joshua Staniland (10)   126
Samantha Jane Lewis (11)   126
Leif Sutton Williams (10)   127

Mordiford CE Primary School, Mordiford

Joseph Rickson (10)   127
Stefan Minett (10)   128
Jack Tinker (9)   129
Hannah Goulding (10)   130
Lucy Abbiss (10)   131
Robert Gardner (10)   132
William Price (9)   132

Ashley Holmes (10) 133
Charlie Hodges (10) 133
Alison Gardner (9) 134

Newton Burgoland School, Newton Burgoland

Joshua Carr (8) 134
Jack Evans (9) 135
Abigail Williamson (7) 135
Laura Coleman (10) 136
Drew Fores (8) 136
Nicholas Robinson (7) 137
Rameeka Banning (9) 137
Tom Evans (10) 138
Jack Spencer (7) 138
Hannah Robinson (11) 139
Daniel Glithero (10) 139
Amelia McCausland (10) 140
Bethan Jacka (9) 140
Sarah Davies (10) 141

Pinfold Street JMI School, Darlaston

Andrew Ward (11) 141
Serena Sansara (9) 142
Kara Page (10) 142
Emma Rollason (10) 142
Akaash Ram (9) 143

Portleven School, Portleven

Sam Orchard (11) 143
Paris Penhaligon (11) 143
Carl Betts (10) 144
Zoe Davies (11) 144
Jowan Shanberg (10) 145
Gemma Harding (10) 145
Will Dawson (11) 146
Kerensa Lewis (11) 146
Katie Evans (11) 147
Lamorna Newman (9) 148
David Ferris (11) 149
Evie Hayman (10) 149

St Martin's CE Primary School, Bilston

Josh Shepherd (10)	150
Louis Pullen & Adam Stokes (11)	150
Mitchell Pearson (10)	151
Toni James (11)	151
Kirsty Brown (10)	152
Natasha Laithwaite (10)	152
Shannon Edwards (8)	153
Lauren Jackson (11)	153
Jamie Guest (11)	154
Kai Sadler (11)	154
Billy Henderson (10)	154
Wayne Lees (11)	155
Gemma Green (11)	155
Curtis Nicholls	155
Jemma Mansell (10)	156
Leanne Tanner (10)	156
Shannon Salter (9)	157
Aaron Asprey (9)	157
Paige Strong (10)	158
Aaron Modi (9)	159
Jade Alder (9)	160

Sutton-In-Craven CP School, Keighley

Hannah Compton (11)	160
Callum Thomas (10)	161
Shannon Cassidy & Naomi Tennant (11)	162
Esther Liu (8)	162
Emma Lang (9) & Rosie Bonser (10)	163
Benjamin Fletcher (9)	163
Rebecca Brown (10)	164
Catherine Walker (10)	164
Kaya Whitehead (10)	165
Ashley Colman (10)	165
Adam Birks (10)	166
Daniel Kirk (10)	166
Aaron Tattersall-Jarvis (10)	166
Amelia McManus (8)	167
Christopher Town (10)	167
Holly Greenwood (10)	167
Sarah Winter (9)	168

Jacob Uren (9)	168
Thomas Mortimer (9)	168
Katy Lloyd (10)	169
Bethany Wild (9)	169
Johnathan Wilkinson (10)	169
Emily Edgar (11)	170
Oliver Robertshaw (9)	170
Fern Worsencroft (9)	170
Ella Beaumont (10)	171
Georgina Robinson (11)	171
Alex Blackie (10)	171
Rebecca Dunwell (11)	172
Sian Butler (11)	172
Stacey Dwyer (10)	172
Joseph Buffey (8)	173
Alessandro De Vito (10)	173
Louise Marratt (11)	173
Becky Simpson (9)	174
Adam Stares (9)	174
Jude McManus (11)	174
Stephen Ettery (9)	175
Daniel Lovell (8)	175
Angela Hayton (11)	175
James Beaumont (8)	176
Josh Waller (8)	176
Harris Catley (9)	176
Ashley Hollings (8)	177
Louise Grace Hinchcliffe (8)	177
Laura Feather (9)	177
Jake Cawthorne (9)	178
Rachel Hargreaves (8)	178
Stefan Grant (8)	179

Trinity Croft CE (A) J&I School, Rotherham

Catherine Tupling (10)	179
Alex Atkinson (10)	179
Aaron Kirkby (9)	180
Danielle Booth (10)	180
Kelly Schofield (10)	180
Dea Skidmore (11)	181

Whitminster CE Primary School, Whitminster

Harry Cowley (11)	181
Ryan Clark (9)	181
Charlotte Parcel (10)	182
Victoria Thomas (10)	182
Millie Lander (10)	183
Nicolas Edwards (10)	183
Lorna Clague (10)	184
Kristian Cheshire (11)	184
Toby Gray (10)	185
Tierney Powell (10)	185
Leanne Williams (9)	185

Ysgol Iau Abergwaun, Fishguard

Nicolle Youngs (10)	186
Danielle Davies (9)	186
Charlotte Harries (9)	187
Kirsten Jenkins (11)	187
Naomi Khan (9)	188
Ruth Evans (10)	188
Adam Davies (9)	189
Gareth Rhys Owen (7)	189
Esther Phillips (9)	190
Rhys Tyrrell (9)	190
Ruth Jenkins (11)	191
Elen Rees (9)	191
Rhianna Chilton (11)	192
Chloe Williams (10)	192
Philippa Jullien (11)	193
Natasha Lewis (11)	193
Sophie O'Connor (10)	194
Abigail Dunn (10)	195
Sam Phillips (10)	195
Chloe Sinnott (10)	196
Lauren Thomas (9)	196
Callum MacLeod (9)	197
Isabel Dunn (8)	197
Matthew Morgan (10)	198
Jessica Tannahill (10)	198
Angharad Portch (9)	199
Lauren Bell (9)	200

The Poems

Friendship

it's a walk in the park
it's a vacation
it's a helping hand
it's my favourite location

it's a Christmas dinner
it's a swim in the sea
it's a special day
it's a cup of tea

it's having fun
it's something to say
it's something to share
it's a holiday.

Jake Carden (7)

Winter

W et dog coming in from the snow
I cicles hanging from the roof
N ests empty at this time of year
T ea in hand, sitting by the fire
E ating roast turkey at Christmas
R olling snowballs to make snowmen.

Chloe Baillie (9)

Cold Ocean

C old, icy, rocky mountain
O cean with stone near it
L ake is so enormous
D ark, deep river.

Sam Ainsworth (8)

Go Away Winter

It is really cold,
There's ice and snow all around,
Snowballs and snowmen are here to stay,
Christmas is coming soon,
Rain is falling,
I am happy,
Get some hats and scarves,
The season to be cold is here.

Spring, hurry up and come,
It's cold,
There are no flowers,
No sun and it's no fun.

Larissa Kerr (10)

Pocket Money Poem

P lenty of choice
O nly so much to spend
'C ause I'm giving money to pay the rent
K eep in saving more and more
E ven too much to burst the door
T icket by ticket

M oney by money
O nly so much to spend
N o more pocket money
E ven not a penny to buy a sweet
Y et still paying the rent.

Emma Muldoon (10)

Winter's Ghost

Winter is a creeping ghost,
Going from host to host.
Winter's ghost goes up and down town,
Crushing leaves and freezing webs.
Winter goes across the sea,
Scaring sailors, ha, ha, hee!
Winter is the ghost of frost,
Made from ice sea and rock.
Winter goes through the woods,
Freezing up webs and oak.
Winter's face, ghost and soul,
Is made from ice sea and cold.
Winter comes to you your house,
Freezing up every home.

Obaidah Sheikh (10)

My Rabbit

I have a rabbit called Hunny Bunny.
He jumps and skips, it is so funny.
While nibbling the grass and running around
The birds swoop down and pinch his bread.
He likes to push a ball with his head
And when he's finished
I shout, 'Get back in your bed.'
I open his cage and shout him in
But he runs off behind the bin.
Birds fly in his cage and pinch his food.
I think they're in a cheeky mood.

Danielle Rayment

War Is Death

People dying,
People killing,
Children crying,
People all around crying and fighting.
Why is the there such a thing as war?

Fountains of blood,
Rivers of blood,
Lakes of blood,
All over the country mothers and wives upset.
Why is there such a thing as war?

Guns being shot,
Sirens being heard,
Soldiers marching,
Everyone around frightened to hear gunshots.
Why is there such a thing as war?

War is not to laugh about,
War is not a computer game,
War is not a TV programme.
    War is war!
Why is there such a thing as war?

Niall Evans (11)

Don't You Dare Touch My Bear

I had a kettle,
It was made of metal.
It boiled my bear
Till it had no hair.
So don't you dare touch my bear!
Or I will throw you into a pond of nettles!

Abdullah Ahmed (8)

The Rocking Reds

Red is the hottest of them all.
Red can be a volcano with
Lava firing down the sides.
Red could also be volcanic ash.
Imagine
Volcanic ash burning
Down everything in its path.
Red is red sandstone
Which the Egyptians made their
Pyramids with.
Red is a warning and an
Alert to stop cars and lorries from crashing!
Kaboom!
Red makes me smile,
I like being happy.
Red could be the dying of blood
Like this part of the poem.

Rory Kelham (9)

Somewhere In Our School Today . . .

Confused infants are happily rehearsing an exciting show
Whilst thinking and forgetting what they're supposed to say.
Year 6 are quickly scribbling down difficult sums
Whilst listening to the teacher's next instructions.
The Year 1s are engrossed with painting 'works of art'
And proudly showing it to class,
Whilst Year 3 are tiredly coming back from break,
Slipping, skidding on the invisible ice.
And last, but not least, Mr Brown's class is singing light-heartedly,
Looking and singing the heavenly text.

Alice Morgan (10)

Hallowe'en

Every time you see a ghost,
You just have to stare.
They make a noise,
Create pain,
They make a nightmare.

Sometimes you see a vampire,
Blood drips everywhere,
He will talk you into a *kiss*,
Dig into your neck
And then he will take you to his lair.
Beware!

Rarely you will see a skeleton,
Bones are on the run.
He will do a little jig,
Chase you all the way,
Until, finally, the sun comes out to play.

Occasionally you will see a witch,
Warts there to scare.
She will introduce you to a dead drink,
Poison everywhere.
As soon as you take a sip,
You will be out in the air.

Every Hallowe'en a spook will come to your door,
Different creatures wander,
Daring to kill.
Don't make a sound,
You're in a crazy town,
Or you will make war.

Seetal Patel (12)

Prisoners Of War

People who kept prisoners of war
Were evil monsters and nothing more
They tortured and starved innocent men
Then when they'd finished they'd start again.
People who kept prisoners of war
Were evil monsters and nothing more.

People who kept prisoners of war
Were evil monsters and nothing more.
If they thought people were going to escape
They'd call out names and interrogate.
People who kept prisoners of war
Were evil monsters and nothing more.

People who kept prisoners of war
Were evil monsters and nothing more.
Interrogation was the worst scare
They'd injure the prisoners but wouldn't care.
People who kept prisoners of war
Were evil monsters and nothing more.

People who kept prisoners of war
Were evil monsters and nothing more.
The English troops barged in and then
Ordered them to hand over their men.
The war was over, the prisoners were free
So they could see their friends and family.
People who kept prisoners of war
Were evil monsters and nothing more.

Bethany Kerr (10)

Trespassers

The sea is howling, roaring with fear,
Trespassers are entering the beach,
They're coming near.
The sea creatures' fear is growing worse,
Who will throw things in the sea first?
People come every night to throw things in the sea,
Spoiling the sea creatures' place to be free.
The waves are growing worse, upset and sad,
Not long until they will be going mad.
The sea comes up and looks at the beach below,
Warning the people it's time to go.
The people are calm and they always say,
'We only come here at night to play.'

Lauren Barbara Mejer Garbett (9)

Flowers

A shoot pushing through the ground desperate to see light
A magical rainbow opening up
The bees charging and snatching the pollen
A dancing head nodding in the breeze
A never-ending smile.

Kayleigh Davidson (10)

Dolphins

Through shade upon shade of aquamarine
and sapphire set burnished gold,
hand upon helpful fin,
and skin so silky in joyful waters
with graceful strength,
I would swim with gentle dolphins.

Naomi Parker (11)

Me

Rainy as a raindrop,
Stormy as the sea,
Wonderful as a waterfall,
That makes me.
Fragile as a flower,
Buzzy as a bee,
Amazing as an ant,
That is me.
Big as an air balloon,
Small as the smallest shell,
Faint as the faintest shout,
That's what I'm about.

Holly Williams (8)

I Saw

I saw a mum making gravy
I saw my dad going in the navy.
A saw a man making bread
I seen someone breaking their leg.
I saw people making a gang
I went to a door and rang.
I saw an apple in a pie
I said to my mum, 'Goodbye.'

Ciarán Evans (9)

Sharkey

Look at Sharkey go
as he glides through the sea
in the race with all the fish
as happy as can be!

William Jones (8)

Rabbie

The excitement of Christmas filled the air,
That morning with you I will share.

Presents piles beneath the tree,
One of them the one for me.

The time had come, the wrapping fell,
There he sat, so neat and well.

His fur so fluffy, soft and clean,
The finest rabbit ever seen!

My smile spread from ear to ear,
I am so glad that he is here.

A creamy toffee, a cuddly ball,
For him a name that I will call.

Nothing posh, nothing shabby,
Just plain old *Rabbie.*

Poppy Ralph (10)
Beaudesert Park School, Minchinhampton

Dolphins Of The Deep

The sea opens for the speeding shadows,
As they race through the inky-black waters,
Moving together as one,
Upwards towards the light,
Breaking upon the surface,
Water dripping off their backs,
And reflecting in the sunlight.
They touch, briefly crossing each other,
Before falling back into the depths of
The ocean.

Amelia Scott-Hopkins (10)
Beaudesert Park School, Minchinhampton

The Door Of My Memory

The door of my memory swung open,
Sunshine burst in.
My eyes gleamed,
My heart thumped,
My mind swirled.
Beyond the vast arch,
Where plants hung waving in the wind,
A sandy patio sat,
Decked with terracotta pots,
Clutching solid stems of exotic Aloe Vera,
With its harsh spikes, scowling.
A coarse-handed man,
With a warm smile,
Played a steel drum.
Emotion whistled through the beat.
Melodious tunes flew across the clear sea,
Before disappearing into silence.
The door of my memory swung shut.

Sophie Theakston (11)
Beaudesert Park School, Minchinhampton

Just A Memory

The day she died,
I was imprisoned at school.
Locked up,
Away from it all.

We buried her
Under a willow tree.
It droops,
Like me.

And now she's simply a memory.

Nettle Grellier (10)
Beaudesert Park School, Minchinhampton

Kenya Memories

In Africa, where the elephants dance,
And the monkeys swing in trees.
And hippos swim in water cool,
And leaves blow in the breeze.

In Africa, where the plains are bare,
But the wildlife's all around.
In Africa, where the lions roam free,
Where zebra, gazelle and antelope bound.

In Africa, where the palm trees grow,
And there are beaches wide and clear.
In Africa, where my memories lie,
All the recollections I hold dear.

Kitty Graham
Beaudesert Park School, Minchinhampton

Rain

Down, down, down
Like a nightly hammer.
Pouring,
Pelting,
Lashing,
Dashing,
This storm is rushing,
'Til all is damp and wet and still,
Umbrellas rise,
Coats appearing,
Waiting, watching,
For the clear.
Why won't the sun come out to play?
We're stuck indoors all day.

Nicholas Womersley (9)
Beaudesert Park School, Minchinhampton

My Puddle

Once there was a puddle,
In the middle of my drive,
It rippled in the wind,
As if it were alive.

On hot days in summer,
I used to paddle and jump,
It turned to watery mud,
As I landed with a thump.

Often in the winter chill,
I used it as a slide,
Slipping, skating, gliding,
Better than a fairground ride.

Katherine Dauncey (10)
Beaudesert Park School, Minchinhampton

Our Sun

Sun, you are so beautiful,
Sun, you are so bright,
You help our world grow,
When you give it light.

Your golden yellow is a beautiful colour,
And you light up our way as we go along,
As we run in the long grass,
While you shine so strong.

Gabriella Rose (9)
Beaudesert Park School, Minchinhampton

A Summer's Day

Herons watch the playful lake,
Kingfishers swat the fish,
Tiny birds sing in their nests,
Each makes a little wish.

Sounds of music fill the air,
With tiny, silver streaks,
Erupting from the feathered throat,
Of a shiny duckling's beak.

Out there in the sunlit sky,
Swallows thoughtfully think,
Out there in the gleaming meadows,
Content horses drink.

Rushing ants are playing games,
Among the glittering grass,
In the wind, blowing hard,
Mini hurricanes pass.

Among the flowers of a lilac tree,
Butterflies flutter around,
Mice scutter, all over the place,
Whilst making squeaking sounds.

Please rid the world of pollution,
Please let the fruit all grow,
Please let the nature go on living,
Please let all the streams flow.

Lily Haycraft Mee (9)
Beaudesert Park School, Minchinhampton

Ten Naughty Children

Ten naughty children drinking red wine
One got caught, then there were nine.

Nine naughty children eating a china plate
One got badly cut, then there were eight.

Eight naughty children up in Heaven
One thought he could fly, then there were seven.

Seven naughty children picking up sticks
One got poked, then there were six.

Six naughty children got stuck in a bee's hive
One got stung, then there were five.

Five naughty children breaking the law
One joined some robbers, then there were four.

Four naughty children sailing on the sea
One got eaten, then there were three.

Three naughty children were very, very blue
One cheered up, then there were two.

Two naughty children playing with gum
One swallowed it, then there was one.

One naughty child who was called Samantha
Went on safari, then got eaten by a panther.

Edward Rankin (8)
Beaudesert Park School, Minchinhampton

The Dolphin

I see you glistening in the moonlight,
Your silvery back is shining,
As you leap into freedom.

I see you escaping from pollution,
Trying to breathe clean air,
And swim in clean water.

I hear you squeal,
Trying to find your family,
And your lost friends.

I hear you crying and lonesome,
Very sad and tired,
I wonder,
Will you escape pollution?

Julia Young (10)
Beaudesert Park School, Minchinhampton

Pollution

Stop pollution, keep this world clean,
Don't throw crisp packets in the stream,
Put litter in the rubbish bin,
Don't leave it on the side of the road, it's a sin.

Keep our rainforests safe and sound,
Don't chop down wood and sell it for a pound,
Stop pollution, keep this world clean,
Leave our world with a pretty scene.

Laura Bevan (9)
Beaudesert Park School, Minchinhampton

Chocolate Buttons

I put a button on my lips,
then it slipped behind my tooth.
It went all smooth and sticky,
becoming all wet and sweet.
Dissolving as fast as snow,
disappearing down my throat.

I put a new one on my tooth,
the button went fizzy and liquidy.
Then sliding off my tooth,
slipping under my tongue.
Melting as fast as quicksand,
turning into a syrup.

The syrup was all gooey,
becoming as sticky as treacle.
Then becoming like water,
the syrup lost all sweet-like taste.
Losing all the stickiness,
just turning into water.

James Steele (9)
Beaudesert Park School, Minchinhampton

Balloons

'B e careful,' I said to a balloon,
A s I released it into the sky.
'L eave no pollution behind, or
L ater on animals will die.'
O ver some trees it flew silently,
O ver mountains high and rivers low.
N ever have I stopped wondering,
S hould I have let it go?

Kate Knowles (9)
Beaudesert Park School, Minchinhampton

Ocean Storm

Angry, raging ocean,
Water starts to spit,
A stormy sea is,
    Rising
        Rising
            Rising.

Winds begin to growl,
Black clouds fill the sky,
Waves smack the rocks,
    Crashing
        Crashing
            Crashing.

Noise becomes unbearable,
Water's pelting through the sky,
Wind is
    Howling
        Howling
            Howling.

Wind is getting quieter,
Waves are getting softer,
Storm begins to
    Die
        Die
            Die.

Noise begins to drop,
Clouds getting lighter,
Storm decides to
    Stop
        Stop
            Stop.

Katie Burridge (9)
Beaudesert Park School, Minchinhampton

Ten Naughty Children

Ten naughty children fighting in a line
One got knocked out, then there were nine.

Nine naughty children trying to eat a plate
One bumped his tooth out, then there were eight.

Eight naughty children in a plane to go to Heaven
One jumped out, then there were seven.

Seven naughty children playing with chicks
One got scratched, then there were six.

Six naughty children knocking a beehive
One got stung, then there were five.

Five naughty children breaking the law
One got caught, then there were four.

Four naughty children climbing up a tree
One fell off, then there were three.

Three naughty children went to the zoo
One got eaten, then there were two.

Two naughty children eating sticky buns
One got stuck to the ground, then there was one.

One naughty child ran off to Spain
He got lost and he was never seen again.

Thomas Hillman (8)
Beaudesert Park School, Minchinhampton

Chocolate Buttons

I put a button on my lips,
It went round and round,
Then up and down,
It was sweet and sticky.

As smooth as cream,
As soft as silk,
Warm and soothing,
It all happens on my tongue.

It is ever so delicious,
It has a great flavour,
But poor old button,
Fading, fading, fading away . . .

Melissa Tuckwell (9)
Beaudesert Park School, Minchinhampton

Sea

You see fish gliding in the water,
Humans stream down to the rocks,
Waves sweeping over to bring the tide to me,
Boats sailing up to the docks.

Bottles chucked off the side of the boat,
Coke cans polluting and killing the fish,
Litter being blown into the sea.
If I had one wish,
It would be to save the world from pollution.

William Priest (10)
Beaudesert Park School, Minchinhampton

Ten Naughty Children

Ten naughty children chopping down an old pine
One got squashed and then there were nine.

Nine naughty children visiting a mate
One got hit by a car and then there were eight.

Eight naughty children travelling to Devon
One was late and then there were seven.

Seven naughty children playing naughty tricks
One got caught and then there were six.

Six naughty children learning how to drive
One didn't pass the test and then there were five.

Five naughty children rolling on the floor
One fell through and then there were four.

Four naughty children drinking scorching hot tea
One got burned and then there were three.

Three naughty children going to the zoo
One got fed to the lion and then there were two.

Two naughty children playing with a gun
One got shot and then there was one.

One naughty child hijacked a plane
Flew to a desert and was never seen again.

George Campbell (8)
Beaudesert Park School, Minchinhampton

Chocolate Buttons

Chocolate buttons are very round,
As soft as silk is what I found,
Chocolate buttons are very tasty,
My chocolate button in my wasty.

Choco buttons are sweet as candy,
I gave a button to old Mandy
She said, 'How very yummy,
Very nice in my tummy.'

Sweet and sticky, very milky,
Smooth, soggy and very silky,
Choco buttons are all these things,
Choco buttons, a lovely thing.

Thomas Lowde (8)
Beaudesert Park School, Minchinhampton

Chocolate Buttons

I put a button on my tongue,
Round and round it sung,
Soft as butter, sticky as toffee,
I loved the luscious smell.

As sweet as candy, as smooth as silk,
Much tastier than the most nicest milk,
Delicious, tasty, rich and filling,
If my mum says no my tummy's willing.

Mouth-watering like a flowing fountain,
Wishing there was a chocolate mountain,
The chocolate button fading and gone
I really wished for another one.

Olivia Schofield (9)
Beaudesert Park School, Minchinhampton

The Mouse

I hear a mouse shouting,
He's hungry for food.
He didn't have breakfast,
He's in a foul mood.

He's looked in the pantry,
He's looked in the hall,
But to his dismay,
There were no crumbs at all.

He smells something good,
At last there's a scrap.
But when he gets closer,
He sees it's a trap.

He huffs and he puffs
And he heads for the door -
And that little mouse
Isn't seen anymore.

Izzy Arkwright (8)
Beaudesert Park School, Minchinhampton

Chocolate Buttons

I put a button in my mouth,
It is silky like a velvet cushion,
Warm and sweet, smooth and sticky,
Incredible, soft and very gooey,
Yummy, delicious, milky, sugary
Melting in my mouth
Disappearing down my mouth.
It is very tasty.

Sophia Colville (9)
Beaudesert Park School, Minchinhampton

Chocolate Buttons

Soft and smooth, round and round
A fantastic button, what a glorious sound.
Starting to turn syrupy and sweet
While I was quivering in my seat.

Down and down, dissolving fast
I wish, I wish my button would last.
I was very tempted to have another
But they were taken by my brother.

Charlie Newman (9)
Beaudesert Park School, Minchinhampton

Chocolate Button

I put a button between my lips,
Around it went and then it flipped.
Dissolving quickly as it went,
This is bad the money I spent.

Tasty and sweet and all very yummy,
Luscious and smooth, it's all so scrummy.
Soft as butter is how it felt,
Disappearing quickly, feeling it melt.

Isabella Boscawen (9)
Beaudesert Park School, Minchinhampton

Chocolate Buttons

I put a button between my lips,
It tasted so rich,
The sugary, luscious flavour.

It skimmed across my tongue,
Up and down, spinning around.
The mouth-watering and scrumptious chocolate.

Freddie Waller (8)
Beaudesert Park School, Minchinhampton

Chocolate Buttons

I balance a button on my teeth and lips.
It tastes so good that my mouth flips.

It trickles right down to my bony hips.
It tickles my tongue right up to the tips.

I think I am floating up to Heaven.
I'll probably have another seven.

I wiggle my chocolate to and fro.
Oh please button, don't go!

Lydia Newman Saville (9)
Beaudesert Park School, Minchinhampton

Chocolate Buttons

I dropped a button in my mouth
It curled around heading south
Down and down, it was chewy
It felt like something very gooey.

Melting smoothly, softly and sweet
Delicious buttons for me to eat
I began to wiggle to and fro
Oh please, oh please button, don't go.

Christian James (8)
Beaudesert Park School, Minchinhampton

Chocolate Button

Chocolate button in my mouth
Up and down, north and south.

Gooey, tasty and good to eat
My dad thinks it's very sweet.

Jock Jamieson-Black (8)
Beaudesert Park School, Minchinhampton

Chocolate Buttons

I put this button on my lips,
And I started to wiggle my hips,
Milky, soft, smooth and sweet,
It gave me such a delightful treat.

Scrumptious, gooey, sugary and silky,
I don't know how it got so milky,
Flavour rich and very runny,
It was starting to look rather funny.

It is starting to get rather small,
Most of it has completely gone but not all,
Dissolving, vanishing slowly away,
Fading, melting day by day.

Georgia Miles (9)
Beaudesert Park School, Minchinhampton

My Moment Of The Game

Our team is running down the pitch,
They're trying to score a goal,
I'm waiting at the goal mouth,
Swinging on the pole.

The crowd is cheering loudly,
We've just scored number two.
The ball is coming at me,
Now what shall I do?

The ball is hurtling down the field,
The distance is getting thinner,
My moment of the game has come,
Oh no, they've scored a winner!

Jonathan Berry (8)
Beaudesert Park School, Minchinhampton

Ten Naughty Children

Ten naughty children drinking wine
One got drunk and then there were nine.

Nine naughty children for school they were late
One got detention and then there were eight.

Eight naughty children wanting to go to Heaven
One went to Hell and then there were seven.

Seven naughty children fighting with sticks
One got killed and then there were six.

Six naughty children learning to dive
One got eaten alive and then there were five.

Five naughty children on a rugby tour
One got hit in the face and then there were four.

Four naughty children climbing a tree
One fell down and then there were three.

Three naughty children went to shop for shoes
One got stepped on and then there were two.

Two naughty children eating buttered scones
One choked to death and then were was one.

One naughty child playing with a gun
He shot himself and then there were none!

George Jackson (8)
Beaudesert Park School, Minchinhampton

Things About My Class

This is Sally, her best friend's Milly,
This is Dill, he's so silly.

This is Harley, everyone calls him Charlie.
What's up with you Mike, need a new bike?

That's Izzy, she picks her nose.
Look, there's Maddi, she's always in a pose.

Nicola is so funky.
James is such a monkey.

Ann is always climbing trees.
Billy, well, he's got knobbly knees.

There's Henry, he's always in a fight.
Look, that's Jim, in the play he sings 'Starry Night'.

Oh, come on, this is boring,
I'll show you some more
If you follow me out of the door.

Florence Grellier (9)
Beaudesert Park School, Minchinhampton

School

S is for swimming, doing front crawl and diving
C is for *calligraphy* with all the cool writing.
H is for humanities (history and geography)
O is for outside break, tag and climbing a tree.
O is for oceans, countries and continents.
L is for learning so that everything makes sense.

Hector Campbell (9)
Beaudesert Park School, Minchinhampton

The Hunter

The mother cat steps out into the open,
Every part of her body tense,
As she stares into the gloom,
She sniffs the evening's air,
Her tail quivering side to side,
The tabby seems to freeze,
She crouches down low,
Hidden in the long, wavy grass,
Padding forward silently,
Her fur up on end,
She pauses for the pounce.

A flash of lightning,
Roll of thunder,
Rain pouring down,
Prevents the kill.
The angry cat,
Races across the grass,
Screaming revenge.

Anna Lamport (11)
Beaudesert Park School, Minchinhampton

Chocolate Buttons

I put a button between my teeth
It seemed to dip and dive beneath.
Sweet and sticky, as smooth as silk
It smelt like luscious milk.

It's melting in my mouth
Whooshing north and south.
Sticky and sloppy, just so yummy
Down it went into my tummy.

Ben Field (8)
Beaudesert Park School, Minchinhampton

Rhino

Bold and proud he strides through the grasslands,
White horn glistening in the heat of the sun,
Leathery skin caked in dry mud from wallowing in the river,
Oxpeckers sit on his back picking away at the tics,
Nature is unaware of the danger about to unfold.
Bang! Bang!
Two gunshots,
Weork, weork,
The birds scatter and the creatures on the ground
Scurry in all directions,
Thuuuddd!
Rhino is dead.
His horn was his death.
It sits in a glass case in a museum.

Bertie Scott-Hopkins (7)
Beaudesert Park School, Minchinhampton

The Eagle

Graceful wings,
Sharp beak,
Deadly talons,
Against man with guns,
The decision, life or death,
The cackling voice will keep you up all night,
And that body, that stealthy body,
Like a snake without a voice box,
When I am gone it will be called The Explorer
Going with the sound of the guns,
And there is The Explorer, The Explorer.

Charles Carden (7)
Beaudesert Park School, Minchinhampton

No Sleep For The Melvin Family

Zzzzzzz sh sh sh
Zzzzzzz sh sh sh

Which cat shall I catch next?

Zzzzzzz sh sh sh
Zzzzzzz sh sh sh

Crash! Bang!
Tiny ears pricked up,
Binky leaps from her warm cage,
Woof! Woof! Burglar alert! Burglar alert!
Woof! Woof! Oops! Baby alert! Baby alert!
What's going on down there?
Oh no! Dad alert! Dad alert!
Woof! Woof! Binky, back in your cage!

Clementine Melvin (7)
Beaudesert Park School, Minchinhampton

Tortoise

Slowly, sleepily,
Time to stare,
He makes his way across the dry, crumbling earth.
He takes a sniff,
Scaly head twitching,
Then a bite from a leaf,
He moves on, plodding,
Quietly, in a world of his own,
Safe in his heavy armour,
The patchwork of green catches the eye of a hunter
Looking for antiques to sell,
Quickly he withdraws his head and stays as still as a stone.

Luke Henry (8)
Beaudesert Park School, Minchinhampton

The Chameleon

Slowly he ponders his way through the leafy undergrowth
of the forest,
His turret-like eyes flicking backwards and forwards,
Searching for insect prey.
His binocular vision fixes on a juicy fly,
Tongue shoots out and lunch is trapped on the sticky tip.
In a fraction of second it snaps back,
The victim is gone.
Sssssss - snake unexpectedly slithers towards him,
Quickly he changes colour to blend into the background.
He is saved from being lunch himself!

Jamie Penmore (7)
Beaudesert Park School, Minchinhampton

The Grey Wolf

Low to the ground a long, black shape creeps carefully towards
dinner,
Little white lambs skip happily, unaware of danger lurking,
A pounce and a growl,
Baa baa baa baa baa baa baa baa baa baa baa baa baa,
Farmer, farmer with his gun,
Bang! Bang!

Rowland Graham (7)
Beaudesert Park School, Minchinhampton

Squirrel

Beady eyes watching,
A quick scurry,
Up a tree,
Nuts in sight,
Stuff them in,
Oh, glee!

Emily Knight (7)
Beaudesert Park School, Minchinhampton

The Llama

Here comes the llama all fat and wide,
His shaggy coat flapping as he trots into the wood,
His face is bad-tempered,
Not a happy chap,
So disgruntled that he does not spot the tree,
Smack!
Yow! That hurt.
He turns around,
His baggy eyes droop further.

Jessica Priest (7)
Beaudesert Park School, Minchinhampton

The Beaver

Large bottom,
Slow wobble,
River edge,
Quick dip, wooden log,
Sharp teeth,
Nasty nip,
Not friendly!

Michael Young (8)
Beaudesert Park School, Minchinhampton

Rusty Red

Rusty Red runs to a rock,
Crunch! Crunch! Munch! Munch!
Down goes a nut,
Sprint, sprint,
Up the tree,
Sleep, sleep,
Snore, snore.

Ellie Bleeker (7)
Beaudesert Park School, Minchinhampton

The Dog's Death

I was as sad as a man,
Without a heart,
I feel like a play,
Without a part.
My face was full of tears,
My eyes like the sea,
I can't live without her,
I need to find the key.
I couldn't believe it,
She was cold and dead,
I couldn't even,
Touch her scruffy bed.
Now a meal only for one,
Never again a meal for two,
Then I found the shoe,
That she used to love to chew.

Isabel Tanner (10)
Beaudesert Park School, Minchinhampton

The Spirits Of The Storm

Blood punches through every vein,
Water flows down sunken lanes,
As lightning strips the windowpanes,
A dark creature stealthily creeps,
Across the illuminated fields.

Turns his nose to scents on every breeze,
Then moves to a clump of swaying trees,
With every flash he stops and freezes
While thunder rumbles and lightning splinters,
Old dog fox retreats to his den.

Alexandra Wharton (10)
Beaudesert Park School, Minchinhampton

Winter

She came with torture,
Murdered the land,
Freezing everything with one simple hand,
She congealed water, hardened grass,
Froze everything in just one pass.

She comes with beauty,
Made a glimmer,
Sprinkled every atom with a shimmer,
Glittered trees, sparkled grass,
Illuminated everything in just one pass.

She came with fun,
Bucketing snow,
To children a fantastic show,
She made slides, covered the grass,
Whitened everything in just one pass.

Rosie Gordon Lennox (11)
Beaudesert Park School, Minchinhampton

First Holiday

Italy.
First holiday,
in the heat.
Sunbathing,
warm seas,
scorpions
in the grass.
Cricket
on a
terrace.
Italy.
First holiday,
in the heat.

Will Purcell (10)
Beaudesert Park School, Minchinhampton

Jack Frost

He came, he saw, he conquered.
The trees clothed with ice.
The river stopped in full flow.
Frozen with dreaded ice.

He is clothed with ragged hessian.
Treads the night with freezing feet.
Deprived of any possible heat.
He stares with beady eyes.

He changes the wonderful autumn colours
For bleak grey and white.
He reviews his work with delight
And retreats to his frozen lair.

Lydia Rogers (10)
Beaudesert Park School, Minchinhampton

Autumn Leaves

In autumn all the leaves fall,
Gold and crisp they tumble down,
Landing on the soft, green grass.
In the woods the trees stand bare
And in the dark and gloomy night
Their silhouette shines in the moonlight.
When all is quiet and only the sound of the wind is heard,
The animals of the wood come to see the golden leaves
Fluttering down from the towering trees.
They have fun jumping around
But soon it's all over
As winter has come.

Camilla Weston (9)
Beaudesert Park School, Minchinhampton

Where Are The Two?

Where are the two,
That rocked me to sleep,
That checked me at two,
When I woke up and started to weep?

Where are the two,
That smiled at me gently,
That gave me treat too:
A teddy called Bentley?

Where are the two,
That I seek for now?
Where shall I look for the two of you:
In a green field or on a ship's bow?

Where are the two,
From a vast car wreck?
Fighting the impulse to cry for you,
All alone on that very long trek.

Roanna Castle (10)
Beaudesert Park School, Minchinhampton

My Nightmare

The towering trees creaked in the whistling wind
As if they realised I had sinned.
I endlessly ran to get far away
But found I would not escape that day.
They swallowed and chewed me all up tight
And spat me out with all their might.
With monsters stomping around my head
Which made me wish that I was dead.

Sebastian Clarke (10)
Beaudesert Park School, Minchinhampton

Ten Naughty Children

Ten naughty children fighting in a line
One got pinched, then there were nine.

Nine naughty children going to a mate
One got hit, then there were eight.

Eight naughty children going to Heaven
One went to Hell, then there were seven.

Seven naughty children going to the flicks
One got scared by the dark, then there were six.

Six naughty children learning to dive
One got killed, then there were five.

Five naughty children pretending they're poor
One got hungry, then there were four.

Four naughty children climbing a tree
One fell off and broke his knee, then there were three.

Three naughty children playing with glue
One got stuck, then there were two.

Two naughty children making a bomb
One got blown up, then there was one.

One naughty child scaring her brother and sister
She got a shock when a zombie came and kissed her.

Emily Verschoyle (7)
Beaudesert Park School, Minchinhampton

Romans

The Romans run over the grass-covered hills.
Terrorising men out on the field
with swords and shields, bows and spears.
They win the battle after a long fight.

James Boggis-Rolfe (9)
Beaudesert Park School, Minchinhampton

The Doughnut

The doughnut,
Not a jam-filled, sugary bun
But something much more fun.
The waves tumbling on the shore.

The floor moving, a bouncy ride,
The top was open, don't try to hide,
Bounce, bounce and bounce again,
Until my teeth ached with pain.

With trembling feet
And soggy seat,
I clung on tight,
Put up a fight,
The squidgy ring tipped up,
Water hit me in the face
From other boats having a race.

A wild and fun time we had,
It also made me really glad.

George Hunt (10)
Beaudesert Park School, Minchinhampton

The Bus

Hurry! Hurry! The bus is coming.
Run! Run! As fast as you can.
I look left, look right, no bus in sight!
I heard a tumbling, a rumbling.
I look left, I look right, there was a bus in sight!
Right at my heel it was, it was,
Going as fast as a cobra in a bush,
Working its way through the hill mist,
It stopped and I jumped on to a terrible sight . . .

Jack Dalrymple Hamilton (9)
Beaudesert Park School, Minchinhampton

The Snow

I was walking along the forest
As the snow melts at my feet.
The snow, the snow, the snow.

I was walking along the street
In the snow, the ice and the sleet.
The snow, the snow, the snow.

I was walking in the Arctic
With powerful polar bears.
The snow, the snow, the snow.

I was playing in the garden.
Where is the snow?
I miss the snow.

Tom Stafford-Michael (9)
Beaudesert Park School, Minchinhampton

Toucans

Two toucans sitting in a tree
Two cans kicked too far to see.
Two toucans having a bath
Two cans kicked along a path.

Four hawks floating in the sky
Four storks trying to look high.
Four wings hovering on air
One is alone, two make a pair.

Six sausages lying on the floor
Six snails looking for the door.
Six sausages cooking in a pan
Six snails looking for a man.

Lucy van Amerongen (9)
Beaudesert Park School, Minchinhampton

Pond

'Miss, why is the pond water gone?
Where are the glittering fish
And leaping frogs?'
'Factories, my dear.'
'But how?'
'Pollution.'
'But why?'
'Because we want cars, fertilisers, engines, electricity and money.'
'What about the water in the pond?'
'The water?'
'Yes.'
'Well, pollution drank up all the water.'
'What do you mean?'
'It drank up the goodness and left us with this.'
'It did?'
'Yes, my dear, it did.'
'How sad.'

Gabriella Ford (10)
Beaudesert Park School, Minchinhampton

Lightning

It rumbles and it cracks,
From high in the sky,
Finding the quickest route down.
A stream of liquid silver,
What stands in its way, electricity shocks.

Like a winter tree with snowy branches,
Filled with a dangerous light.
It hammers down destroying the calm,
Just a moment of peace before the bolt returns.

Max Brodermann (10)
Beaudesert Park School, Minchinhampton

Where In The Water . . .

Where in the water does the whale swim?
Where is he hiding?
I must find him.

Where in the water does the shark bite?
Where is he swimming?
I don't want a fight.

Where in the water does the dolphin play?
Where does he frolic?
I'd like to bid him good day.

Where in the water does the fish glide?
Where is he racing?
Against the strong tide.

Where in the water does the jellyfish sting?
Where is he floating?
I'd like to meet his king.

Where in the water does the pollution grow?
Where does it kill the animals?
I'd like to stem its flow.

Sophie-Marie Neal (9)
Beaudesert Park School, Minchinhampton

The Dying Fire

The orange embers lie on the heated ash,
The flames are no longer ablaze,
Left is only one single log,
This fire is starting to laze.

The sparks in this fire no longer cackle,
The chimney's smoke stopped going to the skies,
The fireplace returns to stone so cold,
Fire has died with silent goodbyes.

James Baker (9)
Beaudesert Park School, Minchinhampton

Grandpa

This man I knew with thin, grey hair,
His ink-black glasses which stare and stare,
His plump, round tummy, a cuddly mound,
His chuckling laugh with its smiley sound.

This man I knew with huge, checked shirts,
His old TV which was fuzzy and blurred,
His big, huge house which was gloomy and dark,
His little pet dog which would always bark.

This man I knew who would like to play pool,
His huge, spiral staircase which would bend and bend,
His shiny, toy cars which would always break,
His wife's big cakes which I would help to make.

For this man I knew it was time to go,
He was getting old but I wasn't told,
I never got to say goodbye,
It was time for him to rest and die.

Guy Mitchell (10)
Beaudesert Park School, Minchinhampton

Bismuth

What is Bismuth?
A simple mineral.
No,
It is a thing of unbelievable beauty,
It's gold and pink,
Like oil on water.

Stacked up in layers like a perpetual staircase,
Colossal golden squares piling in their millions.

Inside the shining, outer layer,
Lies a bluey-silver sparkling lake.

Hugh Acland (9)
Beaudesert Park School, Minchinhampton

Ten Naughty Children

Ten naughty children playing near a mine,
One fell in, then there were nine.

Nine naughty children visiting a posh estate,
One got lost, then there were eight.

Eight naughty children on a trip to Devon,
One fell off a cliff, then there were seven.

Seven naughty children playing dreadful tricks,
One got caught, then there were six.

Six naughty children stealing from a hive,
One got stung, then there were five.

Five naughty children running through a door,
One got slammed, then there were four.

Four naughty children climbing up a tree,
One fell out, then there were three.

Three naughty children going to the zoo,
One got punched by an ape, then there were two.

Two naughty children looking at the sun,
One went blind, then there was one.

One naughty child eating a bun,
Found out it was poisoned, then there were none.

Freddie Burns (8)
Beaudesert Park School, Minchinhampton

Jumping Horse

The strong, sturdy carrier,
Calmly canters through tall, waving grass.
His long legs thump on the ground,
And hot hooves drum on dry earth.
His glossy, smooth coat shines
As, just for a second,
He lifts in flight.

Georgia Mancroft (10)
Beaudesert Park School, Minchinhampton

Surfing Hawaiian Style

The tropical surroundings filled me with delight
But the surfboard filled me with fright.
I steadily lay on it and swam out to sea,
While savage waves fought me,
Twisting and turning on the back of my knee.
But still I urged on as the tide grew higher,
I turned and stood up beginning to tire
And I crashed over waves one by one,
It was then I realised my surfing hobby had just begun.
But as I approached the shimmering shore,
The tide broke and I crashed on the floor.
At first it catapulted me off my toes,
Into the dark and dangerous flows.
I jumped out with joy and then I knew,
My surfboard had proved me this day for true.

Henry Marshall (10)
Beaudesert Park School, Minchinhampton

The Giant

The mountain was tall,
Soaring above me,
Higher than the clouds.

We hiked up the giant,
Though it took a long time,
We struggled to his summit.

We climbed down the monster,
And stopped on the way,
For sandwiches and hot chocolate.

It was all over,
Just a memory,
But now it has been told.

Harry Saunders (10)
Beaudesert Park School, Minchinhampton

Ten Naughty Children

Ten naughty children climbing a tall pine,
One fell off a branch, then there were nine.

Nine naughty children travelling to an estate,
One wasn't allowed in, then there were eight.

Eight naughty children living in Heaven,
One fell through a cloud, then there were seven.

Seven naughty children watching the flicks,
One touched the screen, then there were six.

Six naughty children learning how to drive,
One got run over, then there were five.

Five naughty children jumping on the floor,
One fell through the boards, then there were four.

Four naughty children playing with hot tea,
One burned his hand, then there were three.

Three naughty children sniffing some goo,
One fell in, then there were two.

Two naughty children chewing some gum,
One ate too much, then there was one.

One naughty child playing with a gun,
He murdered himself, then there were none!

Lucy Rogers (8)
Beaudesert Park School, Minchinhampton

Ten Naughty Children

Ten naughty children drinking wine
One got drunk, then there were nine.

Nine naughty children visiting a mate
One got lost, then there were eight.

Eight naughty children wanted to go to Heaven
One went to Hell, then there were seven.

Seven naughty children playing idiotic tricks
One got told off, then there were six.

Six naughty children learning how to dive
One went too deep, then there were five.

Five naughty children on a city tour
One fell off the bus, then there were four.

Four naughty children swimming in the sea
One just drowned, then there were three.

Three naughty children going to the zoo
One got guzzled by a lion, then there were two.

Two naughty children sunbathing in the sun
One got sunburned, then there was one.

One naughty child ran away from school
Hijacked a plane and flew to Roman Gaul.

Alicia Muir (8)
Beaudesert Park School, Minchinhampton

Ten Naughty Children

Ten naughty children travelling down the River Rhine
One jumped in, then there were nine.

Nine naughty children eating off a plate
One threw food, then there were eight.

Eight naughty children flying to Heaven
One fell through a cloud, then there were seven.

Seven naughty children playing wicked tricks
One backfired, then there were six.

Six naughty children learning how to dive
One drowned, then there were five.

Five naughty children playing by the back door
One ate a poisonous flower, then there were four.

Four naughty children glancing at a bee
One got stung, then there were three.

Three naughty children at London Zoo
One got bitten, then there were two.

Two naughty children fighting over a gun
One got shot, then there was one.

One naughty child on his 5th birthday
Had a tantrum and didn't want to play.

Libby Makin (8)
Beaudesert Park School, Minchinhampton

Ten Naughty Children

Ten naughty children drinking wine
One got drunk and then there were nine.

Nine naughty children throwing dinner plates
One got hit and then there were eight.

Eight naughty children going to Devon
One missed the bus and then there were seven.

Seven naughty children fighting with sticks
One got stabbed and then there were six.

Six naughty children learning how to drive
One had a crash and then there were five.

Five naughty children breaking the law
One got caught and then there were four.

Four naughty children climbing a tree
One fell out and then there were three.

Three naughty children flew to the zoo
One got scared and then there were two.

Two naughty children playing with guns
One got shot and then there was one.

One naughty child decided to change his ways
Now you will be amazed.

Patrick Lindsay (8)
Beaudesert Park School, Minchinhampton

Ten Naughty Children

Ten naughty children playing with a mine
One got blown up and then there were nine.

Nine naughty children playing with their mate
One went crazy and then there were eight.

Eight naughty children wanted to go to Heaven
One went to Hell and then there were seven.

Seven naughty children playing with the chicks
Once got pecked and then there were six.

Six naughty children looking at a hive
One got stung and then there were five.

Five naughty children ignoring the law
One got caught and then there were four.

Four naughty children swimming in the sea
One drowned and then there were three.

Three naughty children looking at the zoo
One got bitten and then there were two.

Two naughty children eating a bun
One ate too fast and then there was one.

One naughty child sitting in a pan
He got sizzled and he was called Xan.

Xan Somerset (8)
Beaudesert Park School, Minchinhampton

Ten Naughty Children

Ten naughty children fighting in a line
One got knocked out, then there were nine.

Nine naughty children going to see a mate
One got run over, then there were eight.

Eight naughty children visiting Heaven
One went to Hell instead, then there were seven.

Seven naughty children playing lots of tricks
One tricked himself, then there were six.

Six naughty children looking at some hives
One got stung, then there were five.

Five naughty children bouncing on the floor
One crashed through it, then there were four.

Four naughty children climbing on a tree
One fell and broke his leg, then there were three.

Three naughty children going to the zoo
One went to the lion, then there were two.

Two naughty children making some bombs
One got blown up, then there was one.

One naughty child found a gun
He shot himself, then he was dumb.

Christopher Bowring (8)
Beaudesert Park School, Minchinhampton

Seven!

Seven slimy snakes
Slithering on the ground
Seven sly foxes
Being chased by a hound.
Seven enormous elephants
Sulking by the waterhole
Seven sizzling fires
Burning wood and coal.
Seven slippery, slow snails
Sliding on the path
Seven petrified people
Singing in the bath!
Seven old women
With walking sticks
Seven chatty children
Playing tricks.
Seven terrible teachers
Writing tragic tests
Seven perfect pupils
Doing their best.

I love seven!

Ciara Mulholland Fenton (9)
Beaudesert Park School, Minchinhampton

The Black Widow Spider

The black widow spider
Small as it might be
Doesn't mean it's harmless
It could kill me.

The black widow spider
Spins webs as soft as silk
To catch rogue flies that flutter by
Or of that same ilk.

Oliver Gardner (9)
Beaudesert Park School, Minchinhampton

Castle

The world goes past
By and by
Sometimes I ask myself why
It goes past so fast.

I remember Sicily
So clear!
A place quite dear
A Saracen castle upon a hill.

A thousand years old and still
Standing on a hill so bold
Overlooking a sea so cold.

The men that built it now are dust
But still the castle must
Command respect from all who behold it.

The world goes past
By and by
But for then
Time stopped for minutes on end.

William Threlfall (10)
Beaudesert Park School, Minchinhampton

The Leaf

The leaf falls from the tree,
It silently swirls around and around.
Like a ghost it glides above the ground,
Through the park, over the trees but,
Suddenly it falls down gently
Into a pile of leaves,
Frozen.

Winter has come.

Jack Roberts (9)
Beaudesert Park School, Minchinhampton

The Monster

Once there was a magnificent monster
Who suspiciously stayed under my bed.
Once there was a brainy monster
Who had a humongous head.
Once there was a furry monster
Who was completely covered in brown.
Once there was a silly monster
Who consistently had a frightening frown.
Once there was a frightening monster
Who had very big ears.
Once there was a big monster
Who had so many fears.

Matthew Saxton (9)
Beaudesert Park School, Minchinhampton

The Kangaroo

I live in Australia in the grassland,
It is very hot indeed,
I am part of a big family,
I have a grandpa, an aunty, little brothers and sisters,
My tail is very important,
It helps me to balance when I hop,
Otherwise there would be a caplop,
My babies are tiny,
Humans call me 'Joey',
Funny name really,
I like plain kangaroo!

Jessica Robinson (7)
Beaudesert Park School, Minchinhampton

Goodbye, My Friend

Goodbye,
farewell.
It is time to go
but I just cannot
let you.
I pray and pray
all night,
so you will not
go to the light.
You have been
there all my life
and now
you are just
a memory.

Olivia Denman (11)
Beaudesert Park School, Minchinhampton

Wet Weather

As the rainy day goes past in my class
I wonder how long it will last.
It's indoor break, it's so wet
I've not even been outside yet.
I want to get out and run,
The ground is soggy, that's no fun.
So much rain in such short time,
The forecast is dull but with spells of sunshine.
Slowing down, it's starting to stop,
I go outside, feel the last drop.

Jan Borkowski (9)
Beaudesert Park School, Minchinhampton

My Cats

Chompsky, now stiff and old,
A dusty cream of warm fluff,
Razor claws and roly tum,
Roaring purr of thunder.

Terror for mice, voles and birds,
Squashing with a massive paw,
Emperor of the house,
Before returning for a night of hugs.

Nifty, the midnight queen,
Coming back quite wet and tired,
Ready to roll in the fresh, warm laundry,
Slender, nimble acrobat.

With dainty miaow and gentle purr,
Velvet paws that pad and tiptoe,
Dark and sooty with eyes like stars,
Loving a cuddle from time to time.

Pushkin, dark, chocolaty velvet,
Softly creeping around your legs,
Playing with your shoelaces,
Purring all the while.

Smooth and silky liquid cat,
Dress him in a baby's bib,
Go to sleep in any place,
Waking for a cuddle.

Bella Haycraft Mee (11)
Beaudesert Park School, Minchinhampton

Ten Naughty Children

Ten naughty children standing in a line
One pinched a bottom, then there were nine.

Nine naughty children every day were late
One got detention, then there were eight.

Eight naughty children floating up to Heaven
One fell down, then there were seven.

Seven naughty children going to the flicks
One got into a mix, then there were six.

Six naughty children going past a hive
One got stung, then there were five.

Five naughty children washing the floor
One threw up, then there were four.

Four naughty children making their tea
One said, 'Had enough of me,' then there were three.

Three naughty children walked to the zoo
One got eaten, then there were two.

Two naughty children chewed some gum
One popped, then there was one.

One naughty child got a gun,
You won't believe it - he shot his mum!

Amy Evans (8)
Beaudesert Park School, Minchinhampton

The Dark Forest

In the darkness of the night,
The moon is shining bright.

In the chill of the night air,
I see eyes everywhere.

I hear a faint scuffling,
And a badger shovelling.

I scan the area,
Just as it gets scarier.

I feel the forest floor,
As I listen to a rabbit gnaw.

Through the tall trees,
I feel a winter breeze.

Emma Clark (10)
Beaudesert Park School, Minchinhampton

Christmas

A white sheet of snow,
The roaring fire glow,
Chocolate, how divine,
Writing Christmas cards,
Line after line,
Bright, sparkling star,
The night magical,
Sleeping silently,
As the sky lies still.

Hermione Russell (9)
Beaudesert Park School, Minchinhampton

Thunder

One hot, summer evening,
Just as work I was leaving,
A black cloud or three,
I spied in the sky above me,
A crash like dustbin lids,
Banging together,
Made me jump into the heather,
Lightning flashes cracked the sky,
Like a holy terror upon high.

Dominic Barrington (9)
Beaudesert Park School, Minchinhampton

My Love, My Joy

I saw it there
Silent and still
The green, the blue
The hills over there.

But then one day
The green and blue
Had red, orange
And purple too.

Homes they bred
And lorries they dug.

My love, my joy
Going, going, going, gone.

A heavy weight upon my shoulders
Or more like great big boulders.

I cried and cried until no more
My love, my joy
Gone for good.

Jessica Evans (11)
Bisley Blue Coat CE School, Stroud

Gone!

Our home has been destroyed
My friends have been trampled on
All we are doing is hurrying across the road
Trying to find a home.
Our homes have been taken over by humans
All I have left are parts of my family
And it's hard enough finding food and water.
I have seen other ants climbing trees
But I don't want to live there
I want to live in my home in the field
But, guess what?
The nearest field is an hour away
And I'm tired.

Sophie Mackie Heppa (9)
Bisley Blue Coat CE School, Stroud

Where Has It Gone?

Into the countryside I stare,
Where is the forest? Where are the animals?
Where, where, where?
As I stare into the countryside
I scream in despair, where, where?
Why did they do this?
Was it some kind of dare?
Where is the forest? Where are the animals?
Where, where, where?
This has given me such a scare.
Where do I go, where, oh where?

Jonathan Webb (11)
Bisley Blue Coat CE School, Stroud

Disappeared

It is my home, gone, disappeared
Standing here it is so weird.

My home is burnt, there is no clue
Where do I go? What shall I do?

The city is loud, the city is bright
The noise gives me an awful fright.

My parents are so stressed
Ever since we moved, they have had no rest.

I go home to where it should be
Cars zooming, that's all I can see.

It is my home, gone, disappeared
Standing here it is so weird.

Ben Jones (10)
Bisley Blue Coat CE School, Stroud

Houses Growing, Trees Going

Where are my brothers and sisters, mum and dad?
They have all been whisked away, not one replanted.
New seeds were sown but not of trees, of houses.
I have seen them grow, one by one.
Never stopping, all gradually getting bigger.
Closer and closer they come to me, never stopping, not one,
Until it gets to my turn, chopped down, burnt to ashes
With new seeds on top, not of trees but of blocks.
Soon not one of us will be left,
All replaced by houses, never stopping, never stopped.

Josh Edwards (10)
Bisley Blue Coat CE School, Stroud

Gone

I sat there crouched behind a pile of rubble,
Watching as the trees slowly, one by one, disappear.
I sleep. Then suddenly I hear a noise.
The trees have completely gone.
Where has my home gone?
Why?
What have they used it for?
I look everywhere.
I wonder if my home will ever come back?
I wait. I keep waiting.
But my home never came back;
Only new houses appeared.

Anika Ponting (11)
Bisley Blue Coat CE School, Stroud

Where's My Home?

Once it was there
But not now
Everything is being knocked down
Even my home
All that was left was nothing
Suddenly
There were these noises
I didn't know what they were
I woke up
Big buildings were all around
My mum
And I were on our own.

Megan Laws (10)
Bisley Blue Coat CE School, Stroud

Destruction

I watch them fall,
I watch them flee.
All my friends
And family.
But me,
Where am I?
And now I wonder why,
I did not even try,
As I watched them fall
And watched them flee.
All my friends
And family.
I do not fall,
I do not flee
Because we're just a memory.
Take me now,
Why should I care?
You've taken over everywhere!

Jennie Batten (11)
Bisley Blue Coat CE School, Stroud

Where's My . . .?

'Where's my home gone?' cried the monkey.
'It's gone!' moaned the rabbit.
'Where's my mum?' cried the hedgehog.
'Killed in destruction,' whispered the bird.
'Where is my nest?' cried the bird.
'Destroyed, everything's been destroyed,' whimpered the bear cub.
'Where's my dad?' cried the boy.
'Died trying to save us,' they all whispered.
'What's that sound?' shouted the boy.
'They're back for more!' cried the monkey.

Tom Mackie Heppa (11)
Bisley Blue Coat CE School, Stroud

Goodbye Brothers And Sisters

They came with fire, they came with saws.
They came with axes and chainsaws.
I could not move, I tried.
I could not move, I am a tree.
I tried to warn them.
I sent vibrations through my roots
But I was too far away.
'Why, when I was a seedling, did I blow to this lonely hill?'
I tried to shout like the humans,
Though I have no lips or tongue.
I rustled my leaves in warning
But what warning ever helps? This one.
They cut down my brothers.
They burnt my sisters.
My mother and father suffered the worst.
The chainsaw sliced through my mother.
She crashed to the ground.
It sliced through my father.
He crashed to the ground too.
'Why can't I die with them? Take me too!'

And I was alone.
I couldn't do anything
But watch my brothers, my sisters,
My mother and father
Dying on the ground.

Men have no hearts.

Celia Garland (10)
Bisley Blue Coat CE School, Stroud

My Home Is Gone

I'm sitting on my favourite branch,
Resting after a hard day's work of gathering nuts and acorns,
I fall asleep.
Suddenly I wake,
I hear the cry of birds and the roar of machinery.
I see trees falling to the ground.
I run as fast as I can.
I come to the edge of the countryside.
I hide in a bush.
A few days later I return.
My tree is no longer there.
Instead of grass carpeting the ground, a thick layer of black stuff,
Covering the hole where I buried my acorns.
I sit there, staring,
My home is gone.
Nothing remains.
I am homeless with nowhere to go.

Lauren Underwood (11)
Bisley Blue Coat CE School, Stroud

I Remember, I Remember

(Based on 'The Green Children' by Kevin Crossley-Holland)

I remember, I remember
Back in the green world
Where I used to relax in soft, green grass.

I remember, I remember
When I entered this crazy, white world
Where the white faces looked down at me as if to say
Who are you?

Shellie Noakes (9)
Christ Church CE Primary School, Coseley

I Remember

(Based on 'The Green Children' by Kevin Crossley-Holland)

I remember, I remember the sheep
as they waddled through grass,
I remember, I remember the green, sparkling waterfall
as it glitters,
I remember, I remember my old mate
that played with everyone,
I remember I remember my mom
that loved me very much,
I remember, I remember the beautiful sky
that shimmered wherever I went,
I remember, I remember the green food
as it touched my lips,
I remember I remember the big green field
where I played all the while,
I remember, I remember the cave
that I got lost in.

Danielle Thomas (10)
Christ Church CE Primary School, Coseley

The Green Children

(Based on 'The Green Children' by Kevin Crossley-Holland)

I remember, I remember the green house where I was born,
The little green window where the green sun came peeping in
                                                    at morn.

I remember, I remember the smell of the fresh green flowers,
The roses, sunflowers and marigolds that bring light to our world.

I remember, I remember the fever on my green brow,
My green spirit flew in the green flowers,
The green snow drifting down from the sky.

I remember, I remember the green fir trees in the dark at night,
The green beans that we used to eat.

Steven Powell (10)
Christ Church CE Primary School, Coseley

I Remember, I Remember

(Based on 'The Green Children' by Kevin Crossley-Holland)

I remember, I remember my house so green and cool,
I remember, I remember that great green waterfall.
I remember, I remember that green warm shore,
I remember, I remember my huge green door.
I remember, I remember the green fuzzy bee,
I remember, I remember the wide green sea.
I remember, I remember my brother's small feet,
I remember that green pole where my friends used to meet.

I remember, I remember the dazzling light,
I remember, I remember the frightening sight.
I remember, I remember the pink face,
I remember, I remember thinking they were another race.
I remember, I remember nine in all,
I remember, I remember him looking like a fool.
I remember, I remember sensing my brother's fear,
I remember, I remember not being able to see clear.

Gavin Kelleher (9)
Christ Church CE Primary School, Coseley

The Green World

(Based on 'The Green Children' by Kevin Crossley-Holland)

As I awoke in a dark cave, with no light, I stood up.
I went to take my first step, but nevertheless I began to float.
A sudden force, it was dragging me in,
Closer to the opposite side of the tunnel.
A blinding blaze got closer, suddenly I was gone.

The light had sucked me in, I didn't know where I was.
I was lost in this strange, green world,
Lost and nobody was there,
Except a little green child looking over me.
I spoke, he didn't reply.
I remember, I remember,
The time when I told the people my true story.

Matthew Ball (11)
Christ Church CE Primary School, Coseley

White Child, Green World

(Based on 'The Green Children' by Kevin Crossley-Holland)

It started as an ordinary day,
The birds chirped merrily,
Then I began to wander through the cave,
An adventure,
But deep down I felt worried, I couldn't turn back,
Then a bright green light blinded me.

I took a final step, I was out of the cave,
Then I saw it,
Just green people,
A green world.
Where? How? What? Unanswered questions,
They just stared and stared.
So I stared and stared.

The years passed,
I have lived a different life,
My feelings were mixed,
I was petrified but now I am mystified,
I go back to the cave
But I can't go back to the white world.

People ask me to tell them my story,
Of how I came to this place,
So people are still asking the question,
White child, green world?

Elli Share (11)
Christ Church CE Primary School, Coseley

I Remember, I Remember

(Based on 'The Green Children' by Kevin Crossley-Holland)

It happened when I was eleven years old,
I had found a forbidden cave.
'Don't go near it!' I had been told.
  But:
Temptation took over me and I did,
I ran full speed into the black and empty hole . . .

. . . I remember, I remember entering that cave.
All was dark at first but then all of a sudden
The cave glowed, a bright, luminous green.
Suddenly I stumbled out the other end, wondering where I'd been.
But that's when I realised . . .

. . . Green this, green that, here green, there green,
Everywhere, everything and everyone was green!
Really, it was the strangest place I'd ever seen! . . .

. . . I remember, I remember a few years later
I had made my great escape!
I remember what I wore, I still have it:
A bright green cape! . . .

. . . I have told all my friends and family,
Though they all say I'm a fool,
But I will remember that trip that was so radically
Cool!

Michelle Stevens (10)
Christ Church CE Primary School, Coseley

I Remember, I Remember

(Based on 'The Green Children' by Kevin Crossley-Holland)

I remember, I remember
The bells that I heard.
They attracted my attention
Sounding like a bird.

> I remember, I remember
> The cave that I came through.
> The darkness of the cave
> It was all so very new.

I remember, I remember
The dark green faces.
Staring at me in lots
Of spaces.

> I remember, I remember
> The colours I used to see.
> It used to be white but
> Now it's green.

Stacey Downs (11)
Christ Church CE Primary School, Coseley

The Day I Entered The Green Land

(Based on 'The Green Children' by Kevin Crossley-Holland)

I remember, I remember,
The days when things were right,
And I remember, I remember,
The last day I was white.

I remember, I remember,
The time I felt alone,
I remember, I remember,
The time I missed my home.

I remember, I remember,
When I first saw the bright green light,
And I remember, I remember,
When I saw the most beautiful sight.

I remember, I remember,
How everything I saw was green,
And I remember, I remember,
How I thought everyone would be mean.

Georgina Groom (11)
Christ Church CE Primary School, Coseley

A Green World

(Based on 'The Green Children' by Kevin Crossley-Holland)

I remember, I remember
Strange faces
New places
Facing me.

I remember, I remember
Being scared
I couldn't bear it
I felt worried.

I remember, I remember
Seeing a green light
It was too bright
All I could see was green.

I remember, I remember
I couldn't stand it anymore
It went on long enough
And then they were staring at me.

Gemma Davies (10)
Christ Church CE Primary School, Coseley

I Remember

(Based on 'The Green Children' by Kevin Crossley-Holland)

I remember, I remember
Creeping through the cave
Heart thumping in my chest,
Never thought I could be so brave.

I remember, I remember
The sudden flash of light
Then I saw a green world,
It was the most beautiful sight.

I remember, I remember
When I felt all alone
With no one there to talk to,
I so much miss my home.

I remember, I remember
When the cave was gone
And I was the only white person,
Just me all on my own.

Stephanie Steventon (11)
Christ Church CE Primary School, Coseley

I Remember, I Remember

(Based on 'The Green Children' by Kevin Crossley-Holland)

I remember, I remember,
The cosy green house,
That stood in a little green village,
And that small green brother,
That I loved to bits,
I can remember eating that green food,
That was so tasty,
I remember, I remember,
That huge green waterfall.

I remember, I remember,
That great big country,
I remember, I remember,
Those great pink faces,
And that wonderful food,
That tasted like gravy.

April Dale (9)
Christ Church CE Primary School, Coseley

I Remember The Green People!

(Based on 'The Green Children' by Kevin Crossley-Holland)

I remember, I remember
The green light at the end of the tunnel,
The bells that chimed in time,
And when my brother gave me a cuddle.

I remember, I remember,
Those green, unfamiliar faces,
How petrified I was,
On that cold day of November.

I remember, I remember,
How helpless I felt back then,
When this happened I was a little girl,
I was only ten!

Pollyanna Scriven (11)
Christ Church CE Primary School, Coseley

Who Are Those Green People?

(Based on 'The Green Children' by Kevin Crossley-Holland)

I remember one hand clutching on
To my brother's red jumper,
And one hand on the wall,
I had tripped over his foot,
Instead of walking I had to crawl.

We were very mystified,
It was damp and cold,
There was a nasty smell in the air,
It was a smell of terrible mould.

When we got to the end of the musty tunnel,
I saw a green light shining in my eyes,
There I saw green people,
Wearing dark green ties!

Georgia Walker (11)
Christ Church CE Primary School, Coseley

The Green World

(Based on 'The Green Children' by Kevin Crossley-Holland)

My home, lost forever, in the pit back there,
As the white world grasped me, I left without a stare,
Now my childhood's strayed, this has gone too far,
My feelings are hurt, this is breaking my heart.

Now I'm looking back, tears trailing down my face,
I've lost all of my family, this is a really serious case,
As I walk down the street, the white world clutching my feet,
I think about the green world, and that to see it cannot be.

Chelsea Davies (10)
Christ Church CE Primary School, Coseley

The Green Children

(Based on 'The Green Children' by Kevin Crossley-Holland)

I remember, I remember,
The house where I was born,
When I was born in the middle of morn,
The small, green window bringing in the green light,
Crawling round the green-dusted floor,
My brother on my side, as green as green can be,
I remember, I remember,
The green, green sea and
Me, me, me as beautiful as can be.

I remember, I remember,
The wolf pit on the floor,
The pink face staring from the hall,
Pot-belly prince staring at us all,
I remember, I remember,
My brother on the floor,
I remember, I remember,
Talking to them all,
My green face turning pink in the wind,
Picking flowers, turning pink,
I want to die thinking,
Just think, think, think, think.

Elliot Rollason (9)
Christ Church CE Primary School, Coseley

It's Summertime

The sky is blue,
The clouds are white,
All the plants have flowers;
The birds are singing,
The children are playing,
There's no rain in sight.
Let's just hope the night is bright -
Bringing even more nice weather.

Lynsey Gronow (10)
Ely Presbyterian Church School, Cardiff

The Butterfly

The little caterpillar turns his head,
And feels the morning breeze,
Looking in awe at the trees;
Slowly he crawls across the leaves,
Looking for birds and bees.
Then he begins to eat and eat,
Nibbling, nibbling all day long,
Listening to the birdsong.
After weeks he's fat and juicy,
Ready for his long, long sleep;
Now we see him sleeping tight,
One morning in the warm sunrise.
Next comes a big surprise!
The chrysalis opens,
A glorious butterfly emerges,
Nature's magic before your eyes.

Timothy Solman (10)
Ely Presbyterian Church School, Cardiff

Riding On A Horse

Riding on a horse is fun,
Clip-clop, clip-clop;
There is Will and my dog Siân,
Clip-clop, clip-clop.
Over jumps and through the water,
Clip-clop, clip-clop;
Giddy-up, giddy-up.
A home we go!

Alice Lock (6)
Ely Presbyterian Church School, Cardiff

Fishing

Fishing in a river,
Oh! It's so much fun,
Going with my grandad,
Sitting in the sun.
So much to remember,
What a lot to take,
Rod, reel and lunch box,
We're off to the lake.
Casting in the water,
Hope I get a fish,
Now my rod is twitching,
Oh! What bliss.
Reel him in quickly,
Feel him fight,
Carefully I land him,
What a brilliant sight!

Matthew Lock (8)
Ely Presbyterian Church School, Cardiff

What Wild Dolphins Can Do!

Dolphins can glide,
Dolphins can slide,
That is what a dolphin does.

They leap,
And they sleep,
That is what they would do.

And they would eat,
And they would greet,
What kind and beautiful animals they are.

They smile for quite a while,
Well, I have never seen them frown!

Charlotte Cowley (8)
Foxmoor School, Stroud

Things I Like

Sometimes when I'm feeling down
The quickest way to bring me round
Is spending time doing things I like
Listening to music and riding my bike.

Banging my drum kit makes me feel better
Or ordering a pizza with ham and mozzarella.

PS2 takes up a lot of my time
So does skateboarding - they say it's no crime.

Pulling stunts and tricks on my deck
As mum shouts out the window -
'Don't break your neck!'

Taking a penalty, hitting a strike,
Mixing on the decks and rapping on the mic!

Shopping for cool clothes, watching a flick,
Eating popcorn till it makes you feel sick.

So these are the things I like to do best,
It beats school and horrible tests!

Jared Old (10)
Foxmoor School, Stroud

Poems

What are poems?
They are words, we think.
We see them, we say them.
They mean feelings to some.
They touch your heart.
They lift your spirits.
You can laugh and sing with joy.
They can make you sad
And cry with pain.
Poems mean things.
Mine would be all kinds of feelings.

Samuel Hawkins (9)
Foxmoor School, Stroud

Roy And The Crocodile

There was a child called Roy,
Who was an unattractive boy.
One day he bought a crocodile,
It had a very greedy smile.
Of course the croc adores to eat,
A lot of red and tender meat.
And if you ask him what,
Is the tenderest of the lot,
He'll say it's neither meat nor ham,
Or bread, butter nor jam.
'The meat I am about to chew,
is neither meat or steak, it's you!'
Now comes the grizzly bit,
Let's not make too much of it.
The croc did eat Roy,
Now that's the end of that boy.

Candice Francis (10)
Foxmoor School, Stroud

The Haunted Chair

As I was sitting down to eat,
I felt a chilling at my feet.
It moved up to my knees and higher,
So I ran to warm up by the fire.
As I began to thaw a bit,
I thought I would resume my sit.
I pulled my chair, sat and then
The chilling it began again!
A haunted chair I did assume,
And moved it quickly from the room.
It's now outside and so shall stay,
Until someone takes it away.

Alice Samways (9)
Foxmoor School, Stroud

Me, Myself And I

Me, myself and I
I ask myself why
Who is this person I am
A real person not a sham

I am a person
Me, myself and I
A person I am
Like a cloud in the sky

It's like I'm in a trance
Or away on vacation
It's like I'm in a zone
Of my own creation

It's like I'm locked up
In a prison of myself
Like someone's lost the key
And I can't get out

Inside I'm screaming
It's like my lungs are about to burst
Outside I'm dreaming
I must put me, myself, first.

Sophie Miller (10)
Foxmoor School, Stroud

Snowflake

It's cold and frosty today
Let's pray for the snow tonight
Today it's white and very bright
The lights are out at school
What a fool
I look so cool
Flying by
On my sleigh
Snowflakes are settling all around
So it's time to play.

Sam Coates (8)
Foxmoor School, Stroud

Sunshine

Sunshine pouring through the boughs of a willow tree
Sunshine whisking waves onto the bay
Sunshine peering through my bedroom window
Sunshine bellowing from the deep blue sky
Sunshine scaling the golden grass
Sunshine twinkling on my aerial
Sunshine flying over the country
Sunshine waking me in the morning
Sunshine flowing up and down the pavement
Sunshine hanging above the countryside
Sunshine glowing in my face.

Ben Holden (7)
Foxmoor School, Stroud

Flames

Flames light up in the pitch
Black dark fireflies flow
Through the air fireflies
Flying in the park
Children say look
Over there!

Aurora Bragg (9)
Foxmoor School, Stroud

Me And My Family

My brother likes to have a fight,
My sister likes to fly her kite
But I just want to be just right.
My dad likes to look a sight,
My mum likes to get up early and bright,
The odd one is my nan who just likes to say maybe or might.

Devon Shirley (9)
Foxmoor School, Stroud

Life In India

The scorching hot weather,
Burning the workers' backs.
The raging, cold storm just about to attack.
Silk and cotton, poor and rich,
As they make their food they get an itch.
They work on and on till their job is done,
But after it was worth a stun.
They were like a spider creating a web,
But it's worth it to make a bed.

Kane Shill (9)
Foxmoor School, Stroud

Hallowe'en

Hallowe'en gives you such a fright,
Hallowe'en is late at night.
All the ghosts and ghouls wake up,
They may steal your precious make-up.
You better find them some special treats,
Or you could be turned into monster meat.
You better not show them you're blue,
Or you might be either monster meat or even monster stew.
Look out, behind you!

Ellishia Francis (9)
Foxmoor School, Stroud

Killer Whales

Killer whales flick their tails,
Killer whales flick their flippers,
Killer whales eat large kippers,
Killer whales play all day,
Killer whales like to stay up at night splashing,
Killer whales like to stay up at night lashing.

Holly Martin (9)
Foxmoor School, Stroud

Please Snow

Snow's been forecast in the next couple of days.
Children are dusting off their sledges and sleighs.
Listen to the radio our headmistress told us today.
If it's bad the school will be closed for the day.
Don't get me wrong, I do like school.
I would rather play in the snow, I'm not a fool.
It's been four years since we last had some.
I remember building a snowman with my mum.
When I go to bed tonight, I'm going to pray for snow.
And by tomorrow, well, you never know!

Shifra Kirby (8)
Foxmoor School, Stroud

My Dolphin

See her bombing through the sea
Teach her how to wave at me.
But she is wild, graceful and grey
Fast and flashy in her play.

Her song is high-pitched, like a bird,
Squeaking, squealing, not a word.
In the waves, light as a feather,
Let us swim together forever.

Charis Wyatt (8)
Foxmoor School, Stroud

Quick

Quick, quick, the dog's been sick
Have you seen, it's runny and green
Josh, Josh, run for the mop
And get some air freshener from the shop
Oh no, the dog's looking pale
I think I'll hide behind his tail.

Joshua Ireland (11)
Foxmoor School, Stroud

Kittens

K ittens snuggled on my lap.
I n the kitchen they pounce and play.
T iny toes tickling me.
T ubby tummy, oh, so soft.
E xploring every hiding place.
N aughty claws scratching me.
S oft and cuddly. I love my kittens!

Carys Neale (8)
Foxmoor School, Stroud

Haikus

In the deep, dark woods
There lies a nice, young fox cub
Waiting for its prey.

Along came a frog
Who sat on a big, round log
Scared the fox away.

Along came her mum
Who sat on her large, large bum
Poor frog ran away.

Billy Gray (10)
Glandwr Primary School, Whitland

Billy The Silly

Billy was my dog
Every day he ran after the flock
Cat got scared
And ran away
Upset, upset I was
'Silly little doggy,' I'd always say
Every day I thought of the cat that ran away.

Meg Spiers (10)
Glandwr Primary School, Whitland

David Beckham

His face is as tough as a rock
His smile is as straight as a block
His hands are big and strong
His arms are straight and long
His legs are rubber like a dinghy
His fingers are flat and stringy
His heart is a burning sun
His stare is like a black nun
His voice is like a crowd
And his laugh is extremely loud.

I am his biggest fan.
PS I want to bend it like Beckham.

Lukas Grafton (10)
Glandwr Primary School, Whitland

Siberian Tiger

S lowly walking in the snow
I creep through the trees
B ecause I'm hunting
E verywhere is quiet
R unning quick
I see
A ntelope
N earer and nearer . . .

T ouch with my claws
I catch him
G ot him down
E verywhere is quiet
R eady to eat.

Max Grafton (8)
Glandwr Primary School, Whitland

The Zebra And The Elephant

Far away south where bananas grow
A zebra stepped on an elephant's toe.
The elephant said with tears in his eyes
'Go and pick on someone your own size.'

The elephant limped away
While the zebra looked puzzled.
He walked to the weighing scales
And only weighed two bales.

He soon realised why it hurt.
He followed the poor elephant.
He caught up and said, 'I'm sorry!'
I wonder if he'll forgive me?

Rosy Stark (10)
Glandwr Primary School, Whitland

Sparky

'Hi, I'm Sparky, the show pony,
I'm shiny black and white.
I love hay, oats and bran,
But don't worry, I won't bite.

Whenever I'm in my stable,
When I'm scared at night,
My rider comes to see me,
Before I get a fright.

Whenever I'm in a lesson,
I'm very, very good.
Some people say,
'Oo! Bless 'em.'

Morgan Halle (9)
Glandwr Primary School, Whitland

Pet Poems

I have a cat in my house,
She likes to catch a juicy mouse.
She climbs up her favourite tree,
And I love her and she loves me.

I have a dog,
His name is Shog.
He likes his name,
Although he's a pain.
He chases my cat,
And I don't really like that.

I have a pony,
His name is Tony.
He likes his ride,
And he walks down the road with pride.

I have a cow,
Her name is Bow.
She likes to feed on hay,
After, she goes to lay all day.

I have a sheep,
Her name is Peep.
She grazes all day,
She also eats hay.
She has a woolly coat,
She has a friend, a goat.

I have a goat,
His name is Moat.
He likes his corn,
But he also chews up the lawn.

Zoey Akroyd (11)
Glandwr Primary School, Whitland

The Crocodile

Deep in the jungle
In Australian land
I see a crocodile
In sinking sand.

I try to save it
With ropes and sticks
Instead the crocodile
Eats them in bits.

Now I can only see the crocodile's head
I'm starting to worry
It will soon be dead.

But then I see
A crocodile in the corner
I think it is . . .
Yes, it's the crocodile's daughter.

She's charging towards me
As fast as she can
But all of a sudden
It's the crocodile's mum.

She's out of the mud
Out of the sand
She's alive and kicking
Licking my hand.

Murali Painter (11)
Glandwr Primary School, Whitland

Let's Ride

L et's go for a ride
A nother adventure
N obody else on the road
D rive, drive, drive

R ide, ride, ride
O ver bumps and down hills
V room! Vroom!
E verybody is having fun
R unning over sticks and stones.

Ben Akroyd (9)
Glandwr Primary School, Whitland

Haikus

I had a big dog
He got stuck in a big bog
Then jumped on a log.

I have a fat pig
Likes chewing on a big twig
His name is Wilber.

I have a fairy
Looks like a small canary
Eats like a canary would.

David Pyart (10)
Glandwr Primary School, Whitland

Netball

N othing can beat us
E verything is right
T oday is the day it might go right
B alls are bouncing
A ll to us
L oud, loud shouting
L ong throws across the pitch

Uh-oh, the whistle blew
Everybody shouted boo!

Gwynneth Evans (10)
Glandwr Primary School, Whitland

Haikus - The White Polar Bear

A white polar bear
Looking for penguins to eat
Cold, wet and hungry.

Jumping in the snow
My fur keeps me warm and dry
From head to my toe.

I saw a tiger
I began to run and run
I ate the tiger.

Jamie Gray (8)
Glandwr Primary School, Whitland

Daniel's Number Rhyme

Number one, I look at the sun.
Number two, I go to the zoo.
Number three, I lost my key.
Number four, I shut the door.
Number five, I like to drive.
Number six, I like to lick my lips.
Number seven, I went to Heaven.
Number eight, I go to a date.
Number nine, I write a sign.
Number ten, I play with Ben.

Daniel Watkinson (10)
Hob Green Primary School, Stourbridge

Early Morning Mail

Through long, dark plains she passes by,
Cloudy steam floats up in the sky.

Mail and post are heading to Wales,
Past the trees birds quietly quail.

As people are still fast asleep,
A girl in bed quickly peeps.

She carries letters for the poor,
Delivers to the man next door.

Stephanie Lucas (11)
Hob Green Primary School, Stourbridge

Hattie's Number Rhyme

Number one, I had lots of fun.
Number two, I went to the zoo.
Number three, I saw a bee.
Number four, I kicked the door.
Number five, I was still alive.

Hattie Weaver (8)
Hob Green Primary School, Stourbridge

Kirsty's Number Rhyme

Number one, I had a bun.
Number two, my mum bought me a shoe.
Number three, there was a bee.
Number four, I shut the door.
Number five, I am alive.
Number six, I pick sticks.
Number seven, I went up to Heaven.
Number eight, I had a friend called Kate.
Number nine, I am fine.
Number ten, I am in a den.

Kirsty Dea (8)
Hob Green Primary School, Stourbridge

I Used To Have A Dog

I used to have a dog
Her name was Ellie.
She lived in an old, green welly.
She watched telly
And she had a big belly.
She goes for a walk and comes back smelly.
You find one dog like Ellie
But you won't get many.

Charlotte McNaughton (11)
Hob Green Primary School, Stourbridge

Jamie's Number Rhyme

Number one, I played and won.
Number two, I go to the zoo.
Number three, look at me.
Number four, knock at the door.
Number five, I like to jive.

Jamie Gilliam (6)
Hob Green Primary School, Stourbridge

Motex

Have you ever seen a Motex?
A dangerous, deadly creature that hunts in the forest at night.
He screams as loud as two iron bars rubbing together.
His fangs are as sharp as electric saws.
The Motex has 100 eyes as black as the night sky.
He sprints like a cheetah with a jet pack at 1,000 miles per hour
with his 20 legs.
The Motex camouflages in the dark, gloomy trees waiting for
his prey.
His blood is as cold as snow that has just fallen from the sky.
His slimy green spots are as slimy as mud in a swamp.
He is moody as an old gran who has just lost her teeth.
His skin is made of foil.
His foil is as shiny as polished gold.

Saif Ali (9)
Hob Green Primary School, Stourbridge

The Plane

High in the sky
While we fly
People buying wine
From the trolleys that come by
Flying away
Today's the third of May
It happens to be early spring bank holiday
Gliding slowly
And over the sea
The plane lands finally
Off we go and now we're free
And here we are in a different country.

Emily Flockton (10)
Hob Green Primary School, Stourbridge

Zoomit

Have you ever heard of a Zoomit?
He has two eagle heads.
He is as colourful as a rainbow in a blue sky.
He has lovely, hairy, blue skin
As soft as a pillow full of feathers.
He has two wings as long as a door.
He has ducks' feet which are like a spider's web.
He moves so slowly like a tortoise plodding across the road.
He roars like a lion hunting for its prey.
He is so kind like an old lady crossing the road.
He is useful, he does all the housework
Even tidies bedrooms.
He is the shyest creature in the world.

Jodie Bostock (8)
Hob Green Primary School, Stourbridge

Matbot

Have you ever seen a Matbot?
It has an eagle head,
It is as furry as a teddy.
He has razor-sharp horns
Which glisten in the sun.
He has duck feet
Which are like spiders' webs.
He has wings like velvet.
He roars like a lion about to attack.
He has fangs that hang from his jaws
They look like an army knife.
He moves slowly like a tortoise in the grass.

Matthew Grazier (9)
Hob Green Primary School, Stourbridge

Spotdraghasoures

Have you ever seen a happy, lovely, helpful, kind and generous
Spotdraghasoures?
She has smooth, furry, comfortable skin like a dog's soft fur for
a pillow.
She goes as crazy as an aeroplane at full speed when she plays
games.
She is more cute than a white, soft baby bunny rabbit.
She is more plump than a pig with 2 bellies.
When she is flying her gentle love-heated wings flap up and down
like a balloon popping.
She has two beaming, gold, shiny eyes like jewellery shining so
bright it is blinding.
She sings as beautifully as a graceful pop star.
Her 6 feathery arms can carry up to 9 children on them.
She skips as far as a frog with 20 legs.
She jumps as high as 13 kangaroos.
Her tiny nose twitches more than your nan's nose when she has
got a cold.

She is as colourful as a bright rainbow.
She is as quiet as a mouse.

Chelsea Stringer (9)
Hob Green Primary School, Stourbridge

The Tiger

The wind is like a tiger,
crashing through the branches,
he looks for his food
as he whistles through the trees,
as blood drips from his teeth
he whispers in the wind.
Finally he falls into a deep sleep.

Kyle Hadley (10)
Hob Green Primary School, Stourbridge

Huggy Monster

Have you ever seen a huggy monster?
It's an animal with one eye like Mikey out of Monsters Inc.
It has a very kind personality
Like your parents when they're treating you
To everything you ever wanted.
He has stripy and spotty fur
Like a zebra who's got the measles.
He's got only one ear because the other one's been chopped off.
He can run like a cheetah wearing Adidas trainers
With jets on the back of them.
He sounds like a strangled cat
Because he miaows funnily.
He might hug you tightly
Like a cuddly teddy bear.
He can talk as loudly as a person shouting into a microphone.
He can sing very well
Like a pop star singing gracefully.

Shelby McGann (9)
Hob Green Primary School, Stourbridge

Slimie

Beware of Slimie
He has three eyes, they are as big as footballs.
The two heads of his are like giant oranges come from the ground.
His four arms can carry six people and are like octopuses' tentacles.
Slimie's legs are nothing but slime and as large as an aeroplane.
He can run as fast as a cheetah with a jet pack on his back.
He is horrible as a ghost come from the graveyard.
He hisses like a cobra after his prey and spits at you.

Kieren Kendrick (8)
Hob Green Primary School, Stourbridge

The Rumo

She has a spiked head like a hedgehog
If you go by her you will be dead and prickled
Do not run away
She will get you anyway
She has a robot body like stone
She is a strong flyer like a dragonfly
She has sharp teeth like thorns
She is as fast as a cheetah.

Paige Massey (8)
Hob Green Primary School, Stourbridge

The Fierce Wind

The wind is a bloodthirsty lion with teeth like daggers,
eyes as shiny as diamonds staring out at its prey.
The wind sneaks behind trees
tears them to shreds with its razor-sharp fighting fangs,
blood as red as fire dripping from its teeth,
just leaving branches to rot.

Daniel Gilliam (10)
Hob Green Primary School, Stourbridge

The Yma

Be warned of the Yma
He has six legs like tree trunks
That thump loudly when he walks
He has got four arms as thin as stick insects
And leaves a dot in the ground.

Amy Cox (8)
Hob Green Primary School, Stourbridge

The Gingig

Beware! The Gingig is like an alien that has one curly tongue.
It has eyes on tentacles like an alien.
The silver is as shiny as gold
And the green is like an old frog.
He is like a motorbike rider with leather wings.
He has a velvet, spotty body like a pair of spotty pyjamas.
The two heads bite like venomous spiders.
He has spiky feet like a ferret.
He flies in the sky like a bird.
He hisses like a snake looking for food.

Leighton Soley (9)
Hob Green Primary School, Stourbridge

The Ronnoc

Beware of the Ronnoc
He is more prickly than a hedgehog
He is so swift he's faster than a cheetah wearing his jet pack
and Nike trainers
His horns are as sharp as razor-sharp razors and needles
His teeth are sharper than knives.

Connor Rose (8)
Hob Green Primary School, Stourbridge

Daniel's Number Rhyme

Number one, I have fun.
Number two, I go to the zoo.
Number three, I lost the key.
Number four, shut the door.
Number five, I can dive.

Daniel Pemberton (7)
Hob Green Primary School, Stourbridge

The Cuddle Monster

Have you seen the cuddle monster?
The cuddle monster loves to cuddle
Like when you cuddle your teddy.
He is as colourful as a rainbow
In a bright blue sky on a summer's day.
He has fur as soft as a teddy bear
That has just come out of the washing machine.
He has 2 heads!
He has 4 mouths as big as 50 crocodiles
Snapping for their dinner.
His 5 legs are as hairy as your nan
When she has not shaved for a week.
He has 6 eyelashes.
He has 4 eyes as small as an apple
That is in the fruit bowl.
Although he can be clumsy
He is as friendly as a little old lady.

Charlotte Bond (8)
Hob Green Primary School, Stourbridge

The Amemot

Have you ever seen an Amemot?
He has round glasses like the moon, as round as it could be,
He is as old as a tortoise who was born in the Tudor times,
He is that wrinkly like your great, great, great, great, great grandma,
He has whiskers coming out of his mouth like an alien from
                                            outer space,
He has round red dots on him like a rash on top of a big red wart
                                            on the end of his nose,
He is blue all over like the blue sky on a sunny day,
His skin is as rubbery and rough as a pointy stone in the sea,
He has 10 arms each side, heaving like snakes' tongues.

Carla Evans (9)
Hob Green Primary School, Stourbridge

Jester

Beware of the devouring Jester.
He squeals as loud as a whistle squeals at you.
He has stripes all different colours like a zebra.
He as 5 eyes as big as basketballs that have just been blown up!
He has 2 mouths.
He has wrinkly skin like a 98-year-old lady.
He has scales that are slimy like a slug's tail.
He has 10 legs as long as a tall daddy-long-legs.

Kirsty Parker (9)
Hob Green Primary School, Stourbridge

A Windy Night

I lay in bed last night
I had a scary fright
'What's that?' I said
Bang! Bump! Thud!
Crash! Bang! Wollop!
Howl! Whoosh! Weeee!
It was only the wind but it did scare me!

Charlotte Portman (9)
Hob Green Primary School, Stourbridge

The Forest

The wind is like a wolf
Searching for its prey
Fangs brighter than the moon
Trees sway in the breeze
Branches breaking off the trees
Falling down on the ground.

Luke Jeffries (9)
Hob Green Primary School, Stourbridge

Chris's Number Rhyme

Number one, I have fun.
Number two, I grew and grew.
Number three, I see a bee.
Number four, I shut the door.
Number five, I can dive.
Number six, I can fix.
Number seven, I go to Heaven.
Number eight, I lift a weight.
Number nine, I drink wine.
Number ten, I say my rhyme again.

Christopher Watkinson (9)
Hob Green Primary School, Stourbridge

Jodie's Number Rhyme

Number one, I have fun.
Number two, I see a zoo.
Number three, I have a bee.
Number four, I bang the door.
Number five, I have a jibe.
Number six, I have lots of ticks.
Number seven, I go to Devon.
Number eight, I shut the gate.
Number nine, I draw a line.
Number ten, I play with Ben.

Jodie Doran (8)
Hob Green Primary School, Stourbridge

Alice's Number Rhyme

Number one, the day is done.
Number two, I have no clue.
Number three, I climb a tree.
Number four, I open the door.
Number five, I feel alive.
Number six, I pick the sticks.
Number seven, I went to Heaven.
Number eight, I have a date.
Number nine, I drink some wine.
Number ten, I have a hen.

Alice Skelding (10)
Hob Green Primary School, Stourbridge

Luke's Number Rhyme

Number one, I went for a run.
Number two, the sky was blue.
Number three, I found a key.
Number four, I bang on the door.
Number five, I dance and jive.
Number six, I pick some sticks.
Number seven, go to Devon.
Number eight, I go on a date.
Number nine, I drink lots of wine.
Number ten, my friend is Ben.

Luke Watkinson (10)
Hob Green Primary School, Stourbridge

Kurtis' Number Rhyme

Number one, I ate a bun.
Number two, I buckle my shoe.
Number three, I saw a bee.
Number four, I kicked the door.
Number five, I learnt how to dive.
Number six, I played some tricks.
Number seven, I drove to Devon.
Number eight, I open the gate.
Number nine, I walked the line.
Number ten, I saw two men.

Kurtis Russell (8)
Hob Green Primary School, Stourbridge

The Howling Wind

The wind is a wolf, whistling in the moonlight,
As it attacks its prey.
It chews with its sharp, terrifying teeth,
He dribbles as he eats,
The wind is a hideous hunter,
Poaching his lunch,
The wind is like a flaming fire burning
With red, yellow and orange.
The wind makes the trees tremble
Until they fall.

Sophie Lewis (9)
Hob Green Primary School, Stourbridge

The Wind Wolf

The wind is a wicked wolf,
A grey vicious beast attacking every animal
And killing it until it's a rack of rotting bones.
It's a swift hunter stalking his prey.
The wolf is like a flawless fire,
Never stopping, always burning trees
Until there is nothing but ash.
The wind is a crafty wolf,
With his globe-like, glaring eyes dazzling like diamonds,
Shining in the sky.

Jordan Tanner (10)
Hob Green Primary School, Stourbridge

The Wind

The wind is like a power
Swaying round and round
Making people go to sleep
To turn them into ghosts
That believe in me!
The house is haunted with wolves and dogs,
They will always respect me
As I am nice.
The witches in the house are as nasty as me,
I'll teach them a lesson
Like they have never had in their lives before they die.

Hussna Tariq (9)
Hob Green Primary School, Stourbridge

The Rabbit Called Izie

Have you ever seen a rabbit called Izie?
She has floppy ears and soft paws like very soft cotton wool.
She is covered in white, glittery fur with baby-blue eyes
Like a baby asleep.
She has floppy ears down to the end of her chin in the sweet,
green grass.
She opens her mouth like a very big yawn.
Her whiskers are as blonde as they can be on her lovely face.
She eats food when she goes to bed in the night like us.
When she runs she runs like a little baby running across the room.
Her fur is white and brown spotty like her ears.
Her fur is like cotton wool.
She eats her dinner in her basket.

Charlie Lingard (8)
Hob Green Primary School, Stourbridge

The Mysterious Woods

The wind is an eagle,
Moving swiftly across the night sky.
Underneath the treetops are fizzing fires
And dazzling diamond eyes.
The fire is like a poisonous gas filling the air
With dangerous chemicals.
The animals are feasting on human flesh,
Leaving the bones to rot.
They hear *boom, boom, boom.*
The hunter is advancing.
They run for shelter.

Laura Edwards (9)
Hob Green Primary School, Stourbridge

The Wind

The wind is a wolf,
Blood so red dripping from the yellow fangs,
Like a pipe full of water.
Trees swashing, brown, horrifying branches
Breaking down onto the ground.
His eyes are like gold diamonds,
Gazing at the trees.
He pounces on his prey,
Ready for the kill,
His fangs like needles sticking into material
And taking the bark off,
As if it was skin on his victim.

Sophie Radford (10)
Hob Green Primary School, Stourbridge

The Whistling Wind

The wind is a tiger,
Searching for its prey
With evil eyes, its soft skin
As bright as a flaming fire.
It's like a dazzling diamond
Prancing around the sky.
It's like a screaming baby
Screaming its head off.
The terrifying trees
Blowing in the wind,
Howling through the night air.

Jessica Rogers (9)
Hob Green Primary School, Stourbridge

The Wind

The wind is a tiger,
All vicious and almighty,
Chewing his food,
Grinding through the soul of the earth.

The tiger seeks its prey,
Twizzling and twirling through the grass
Like a hurricane,
Staring at his bloodthirsty enemy.

It sneaks up at animals,
Chasing them down the fields
Like a creepy ghost
Trying to frighten them into their deadly graves.

Salman Sadiq (10)
Hob Green Primary School, Stourbridge

The Wind's Prey

The wind is a wolf,
With grey, glistening, deadly diamond fangs.
Red and orange fire
Burning twigs off the dark brown trees
Like two repulsive lions
Gnawing through the wood.
Fireworks taking animals to their death.
The wicked wolf growling at the vicious gunshot,
Watching with glistening eyes
At the bright red blood dripping onto the paper-cut blades of grass.

Hannah Horton (9)
Hob Green Primary School, Stourbridge

Windy Wolf and Sky Eagle

The wind is like a wicked wolf howling all night long.
There is the sky, it's like an evil eagle coming to get you.
They're like twins, they're like hunters creeping all night long.
The wolf eats the rotten bones, the body has been eaten by
                                                    the eagle.
They stayed out all night, staring with their shiny, sparkly, diamond
                                            eyes all night long.

There is blood dripping from their mouths
They have had their prey.
The next day they hunted and hunted but no food to be found.
They hunt all night long.
They are so hungry they have to eat the vast, green leaves of
                                                    the trees.

Now there is no more food to eat,
They sadly go away with no food at all.

Stacey Jones (9)
Hob Green Primary School, Stourbridge

Hot Stuff!

Large feathers
Broken tethers
Full of grace
Sets the pace
Shiny beak
Upon the mountain peak
Soaring high
It owns the sky
Put it together
I am a . . .

Phoenix!

Jozef Doyle & George Martin Acton (10)
Lindens Primary School, Sutton Coldfield

Underwater Killer

Sharp teeth
No feet
Loves fish
Not on a dish
Lives under water
Likes to slaughter
Put it together
I'm a . . . ?

Alex Dudley & Mitchell Ball (9)
Lindens Primary School, Sutton Coldfield

4Guess Who?

Human-killer
Spine-chiller
    Great-eater
    Blood-drinker
Boat-crusher
Sea-creature
    Big-biter
    Fish-fighter

Guess who?

Robyn Gough & Lakeisha Sewell (10)
Lindens Primary School, Sutton Coldfield

Furry Face

I am a pet
I don't like my vet
I like fish
In a dish
I lie on your lap
I am a . . . ?

Rachel Huckfield (9)
Lindens Primary School, Sutton Coldfield

It Is A . . .

Lots of hair
Not a bear
A very cute face
Wins every race
Mostly yellow
Not a nice fellow
My best friend is a . . .

Elena Tallis, Heidi McManus (10) & Katie Perkins (9)
Lindens Primary School, Sutton Coldfield

Gone Forever

Very little
I am brittle
Far apart
I lie alone
My song's long tone
Gone forever
Not that clever.
What am I?
Do you know?

Megan Saul (10) & Josh Finegan (9)
Lindens Primary School, Sutton Coldfield

Whiteness

Ice skater
Ice breaker.

Feet basher
Snow wrapper.

Deep sleeper
Fish sweeper.

What am I?

Ben Whatley & Arjan Mangat (9)
Lindens Primary School, Sutton Coldfield

Tom, Socks, Jen And Don

Small and quick
Plays with sticks.
Catches spiders that can give you a fright
And is nearly always out at night.
Up the stairs there is a thud
Oh no, it's got worms in mud.

Do you know what it is?

Samuel James Crawford (10) & Oliver Willis (9)
Lindens Primary School, Sutton Coldfield

Smelly Elle

Gigantic
Never frantic
Grass eater
Never a competer
Marvellous metre
As clever as a cheetah

I am a Smelly Elle.

Katie Fletcher & Emily Freegard (9)
Lindens Primary School, Sutton Coldfield

The Cat

I have fur
I like to purr
I've a pink nose
Paws not toes
I get stuck in trees
And scare all the bees.

What am I?

Jade Morris (9)
Lindens Primary School, Sutton Coldfield

A Spider

Big and hairy
Really scary
Climbs up the drain
Is a real pain
Wakes up at night
And gives you a fright
Crawls in your hat
And ends up flat.
What am I?

Paul Weston (10)
Lindens Primary School, Sutton Coldfield

Furry Face

I am a pet
I don't like my vet
I like fish
In a dish
I lie on your lap.
I am a . . . ?

Nicole Flavell-Avery (9)
Lindens Primary School, Sutton Coldfield

Killer

Heat giver
Short liver.

Hot place
Little space.

It's a killer
Burning shiver.

It's a . . .

Toni Stevens (10)
Lindens Primary School, Sutton Coldfield

Riddler

Four legger
Food begger.

Rabbit chaser
Fast racer.

Hand licker
Tongue flicker.

All rounder
Cat pounder.

Do you know what I am?

Joe Geens (9) & Thomas Strawford (10)
Lindens Primary School, Sutton Coldfield

My Pet Friend!

I am a pet
My nose is wet
I like to roll in the dirt
My owner wears a shirt
My nickname is woofer
And I am a food scoffer
My food goes down in a gulp
And I beat the cat to a pulp.

Can you guess who I am?
Go on, have a try,
I am a . . .

Alison Black & Sophie Fisher (9)
Lindens Primary School, Sutton Coldfield

Wolf Haiku

The wolf howls loudly.
Howling at the moon, howling.
He's restless tonight.

Loren Sawyer (8)
Manorbier VCP School, Tenby

Brother

Messy eater,
Noisy maniac,
Toy destroyer,
Bottle drinker,
Superb fighter,
Nappy nightmare,
Non-swimmer,
Lip kisser,
Bogey picker,
Tree lover,
Peace vandaliser,
Bottle madness,
Water lover,
Night walker,
Kind really.

Kate Harries (8)
Manorbier VCP School, Tenby

Earth Tiger

As she prowls through the rainforest
She spots her prey.
Her cubs are at home
Out of danger's way.
She ducks beneath the long, green grass
And she slyly plods onwards.
Suddenly - *jump* - she grabs her prey.
She is looking very pleased with herself
At the end of the day.

Sally Harvey (9)
Manorbier VCP School, Tenby

Autumn

Autumn is birds flying south away from the cold winter,
Autumn is leaves turning into different colours,
Autumn is Bonfire Night with fireworks crashing in the dark,
Autumn is when the clocks go back,
Autumn is Hallowe'en when the children go trick or treating,
Autumn is conkers falling off the trees,
Autumn is when the sun isn't very hot,
Autumn is when there are no more ice creams.

Rowan Griffiths (8)
Manorbier VCP School, Tenby

Dad

Kung Fu-kicker
Beer-drinker
Loud-shouter
Football-player
Telly-watcher
Girl-lover
Lip-singer
Good-worker.

Tom Grover (9)
Manorbier VCP School, Tenby

Fire

Fire is death waiting for its next victim.
Fire is hot, like a risk to die with honour,
Fire is the Devil's home, home of fire,
Fire decides to kill or let you live,
Fire is not to be messed about with,
Fire lives only to spread,
Fire can burn you and kill you,
Fire can beat you.

Seth Harvey (7)
Manorbier VCP School, Tenby

Water

Water falls like a hand,
Creeping down the rocks,
Sailors risk their lives in the ocean,
They are fighting madness,
Fish are like a community
Fighting against pollution that we throw at them,
Water can be clear like a piece of plastic,
It can be blue like the sky
And blue paint on the wall,
It can be green like grapes
And a packet of cheese and onion crisps,
Reflection like an ocean of mirrors.

Jack Wilkinson-Dix (8)
Manorbier VCP School, Tenby

Mum

Tidy-eater
Tea-drinker
Make-up-wearer
Loud-chatterer
Shop-owner
Daughter-lover.

Ruby Goddard (8)
Manorbier VCP School, Tenby

Dad

Big-eater
Newspaper-reader
Television-watcher
Settee-sleeper
Big-snorer.

Chloe Moss (7)
Manorbier VCP School, Tenby

What Is The Moon?

The moon is a bright ball
　　Rolled onto a black sheet.

It is a newspaper
　　Papier mâchéd into a ball shape.

The moon is a round, steel bin
　　In a dark room shining.

It is a reflection
　　Coming from the sea.

The moon is a white half-circle
　　Cut out on black paper.

Greg William John
Manorbier VCP School, Tenby

Water

The river is cold and deep,
The stream is calm and weak,
The waterfall crashes on the rocks,
The paddling pool looks like a clock,
The sea is strong and rough,
It makes sailing really tough,
The lake is wavy or flat,
The weed is like a mat.

Scott Bevan (8)
Manorbier VCP School, Tenby

Sea Haiku

Swimming in the sea,
Dinghies floating on water,
Having so much fun.

Alexandra Holmes (8)
Manorbier VCP School, Tenby

Brothers

Bath-haters,
Non-swimmers,
Polite-eaters,
Loud-voices,
Mistake-makers,
Book-rippers,
Marmite-lovers,
Butter-likers,
Mum-huggers.

Caitlin Buck (7)
Manorbier VCP School, Tenby

Water

Water, we all jump in the puddles,
Water, we all swim in the pool,
Water is sea animals swimming in the sea,
Water is a nice, cold drink,
Water is in our bodies,
Water is hot and cold,
Water is rain going tip-tap, tip-tap on the windowpane,
Water is lovely waterfalls,
Water, we would die if we did not have water.

Logan Cardy (8)
Manorbier VCP School, Tenby

Earth

The Earth is a big ball
Made up of continents and countries
Floating in space.
The Earth is a giant spaceship,
The Earth is a mystery box
Waiting to be unravelled.

Milea Williams (9)
Manorbier VCP School, Tenby

Music

Music is in my head
Jumping round step-by-step.

The sound of the music
Going down to my feet.

As I use the dance mat
To keep up with the beat.

The tune is almost over
And I need a rest.

I look at the score
And I'm the best!

Emma Grimbaldeston (10)
Manorbier VCP School, Tenby

The Polar Bear

A polar bear wanders through the Arctic,
Padding on snow, wild and bejewelled,
Making his way through the tough, bitter blizzard.
Desperate to get home to his burrow under the snow.
His coat, glossy and magnificent . . . ripply and sleek.
He finds his burrow and climbs into it,
Getting away from the frosty atmosphere,
Delighted to be back in his cosy bed,
Snug and warm.

Aniya Louise Thornton (10)
Manorbier VCP School, Tenby

Water

Water is everywhere,
Water is powerful,
Water can kill you,
Water gives us life.

Jonathon Morris (8)
Manorbier VCP School, Tenby

What Is The Moon?

The moon is a big ball
floating around in space.

The moon is a big ball
made of cheese sitting in a dark fridge.

The moon is a beach ball
waiting to get kicked around.

The moon is the shape of your nail on your finger
after you trap it in a door
and it has gone black.

What is the moon?

Rebecca Williams (10)
Manorbier VCP School, Tenby

Sun

The sun shines on me,
It takes my bad feelings away,
I like the sun for making me happy,
The sun shines on me,
I get the feeling I am the sun,
But I'm not!

Chloe Lewis (7)
Manorbier VCP School, Tenby

Water

Water's wet, water's cold,
A waterfall, a water spout,
Two whales in the water,
Every day water falls,
Rain drizzling outside.

Holly Walker (8)
Manorbier VCP School, Tenby

The Earth

The Earth is yours, the Earth is mine,
The Earth is where you and I live,
The Earth is where thousands of us die,
The Earth is where thousands of us are born.

The Earth has many mysteries
For you and me,
You can't just get a golden key
And unlock all the Earth's secrets.

The Earth is kind,
The Earth is mean,
The Earth is ugly,
The Earth is pretty,
The Earth is funny,
The Earth has money.

Places for you to find,
So go out and find your destiny.
Tell all the world
What you think
About the world.

Lloyd Davies (10)
Manorbier VCP School, Tenby

What Is A Cloud?

The cloud is a big bubble
Waiting to rain.

It is a grey cloud
Waiting to make a puddle.

A cloud is something
That makes people get their washing in.

It is a grey object
That lives up in the sky.

Roxanne Walker (11)
Manorbier VCP School, Tenby

Time

Time, draining our lives away,
Silently taking us one step closer
To the trap of death every day.

Time, only it can put us to bed,
Still there,
Even at the earliest of dawn.

Time, that little tick-tock aging us all,
Disguised in attractive,
Colourful clocks.

Time, the unracable killer.
Time, the every life filler.
Time, the unstoppable.

It's always there,
Don't stop to stare,
Just use your life,
Yourself.

Sarah Giffard (11)
Manorbier VCP School, Tenby

What Is The Sea?

The sea is a conqueror
Waiting to take the land by storm.

It is an empire
Biding its time to expand.

The sea is a mystery box
With many secrets untold.

It has guardians
Which you can't believe are true.

The sea has powers
Beyond your wildest dreams.

George Scott (10)
Manorbier VCP School, Tenby

What Is A Moon?

The moon is a white chocolate cone
placed on a black piece of paper.

It is white rock ball
waiting to explode.

The moon is a white circle cut out
waiting for the sun to go down to show its good looks.

It is a stone all mushed together
to create the *moon.*

The moon is a cheese ball
floating in the sky.

Sophie Wilson (10)
Manorbier VCP School, Tenby

Green

Green is the colour of the bellowing sea,
As it thrashes to and fro,
Green is the colour of our favourite tree,
Green is the colour of my home tea,
As it fills me with warmth and glee.

Abi Markham (11)
Manorbier VCP School, Tenby

Limerick

There once was a lady from Leeds,
who ate a packet of seeds.
She had flowers on her head,
and grass in her bed
and her body was covered in weeds.

Jack Grover (10)
Manorbier VCP School, Tenby

The Moon Is . . .

The moon is
a big ball of dust in the sky.

The moon is
a big light to light up the sky.

The moon is
a big, round ball of cheese.

The moon is
A cat's eye flashing in the dark.

The moon is
a symbol in the sky.

Josh Noott (9)
Manorbier VCP School, Tenby

Purple

Purple is danger coming towards me.
Purple is a colour of the rainbow
And bats flying through the night sky.
Purple is the opposite of pink.
Purple is the colour of a bag.
Purple is the colour of paint.
Purple is the colour of a T-shirt.
Purple is the colour of a pair of trousers.

Aimee May Lewis (9)
Manorbier VCP School, Tenby

Earth

The Earth is a ball floating in space,
It looks like someone's smiling face.

Charley Aspley (8)
Manorbier VCP School, Tenby

Louisa

Louisa, I love you
That much is true
But the question is
Do you love me too?

You make my life
Complete and you are
More sweet
Than a sweet.

Louisa, you're my lovely dove
And you look like
An angel
From Heaven above.

Joshua Staniland (10)
Manorbier VCP School, Tenby

Holidays

Holidays are fun.
Holidays are very grand.
All day in the sun.
Playing in the sand.

Ice cream and lollies.
Gulls by the sea.
Mum with a camera
But she can't see me.

Dad in the water.
My brother plays in the sand.
I like holidays.
Aren't they grand?

Samantha Jane Lewis (11)
Manorbier VCP School, Tenby

D-Day

You are in a boat shivering and vomiting out of it
Then explosions everywhere
You are frightened
Then the door opens
Your friends get shot in the first second
You jump out of the boat
Quickly you are in the water
There is blood everywhere
You run on to the beach and into the foxhole
Then you feel a pain in your chest
You are drowsy and tired
Then you see a light
You are coming closer to the light
Closer, closer, closer.

Leif Sutton Williams (10)
Manorbier VCP School, Tenby

Life In The Sky

I'm a high wing fighter
Soaring in the sky.
Flying past German fighters
Bullets, a flickering light.
Fire as red as blood
Smoke as black as death.
The sun in your eyes
Like an angel.
I'm hit!
Heart pounding
Falling, I can't breathe.
All the achievements
My family.
The pain it brings to my heart.
My life is over.

Joseph Rickson (10)
Mordiford CE Primary School, Mordiford

Man Utd

Man United winnin'
Keane's kickin'
Ronaldo's trickin'
Giggs' missin'
Howard savin'
Djemba Djemba volleyin'
Nistelrooy scorin'
Scholes' headerin'
Fergie boot blastin'
O'Shea tacklin'
Forlan top strippin'
G Neville throwin'
Solskjaer slippin'
Nistelrooy divin'
Kleberson whackin'
Keane's killin'
League winnin'
Wenger's disappointed.

Stefan Minett (10)
Mordiford CE Primary School, Mordiford

Mouse

Mouse
leaps in a bush,
scrambles up a tree,
hops like
a grasshopper
and scurries up your knee.
It hides
like a shadow,
and it's very
hard to see.
It crawls
along
the
floor
and
goes
bee.   as
a   fast
as

Jack Tinker (9)
Mordiford CE Primary School, Mordiford

In My Garden

When I go in the garden,
It's like a different world,
Looking at the flowers,
Shaped straight, round and curled.

Sitting in my garden,
Watching bugs and bees,
Listening to the birds,
That are singing in the trees.

Planting out some pansies,
Then each day watch them grow,
Growing bigger and bigger,
Swaying to and fro.

Now it's getting dark,
Birds tweeting goodnight,
I'll just have to wait
Until the morning light.

Hannah Goulding (10)
Mordiford CE Primary School, Mordiford

It's A Bird's Life

Sparrows collecting sticks
for making cosy nests,
blue tits eating seeds
while perching for a rest.

Thrushes hopping round
pecking for some moss,
the other bird is watching her
showing her who's boss.

Tree creepers creeping
up the big, oak tree,
looking on the ground
to see what he could see.

Now the day is over
what a happy day it's been,
just think of all the birds
that both my eyes have seen.

Lucy Abbiss (10)
Mordiford CE Primary School, Mordiford

The Soldier

My tombstone is upon me,
I'm sleeping in the ground,
My body's in a coffin,
My destiny is bound;
The graveyard is quiet,
No one can hear a sound,
My spirit's in the clouds,
I am sleeping, sleeping in the ground.

No more bullets firing,
No more gunpowder spilt,
No more cannons blasting,
No more fuses lit,
No more soldiers dying,
There are only tombstones,
Where brave men once stood.

Robert Gardner (10)
Mordiford CE Primary School, Mordiford

The Twinkling Star

The twinkling star shines very far
It twinkles all night.

It's very, very bright
It shines above us.

It shines and glows
Like the wind blows.

Look up at the sky
To look for the star in your car.

Most of all
Look for the star at Christmas.

William Price (9)
Mordiford CE Primary School, Mordiford

Mordiford Football Team

Ben Parks headerin'
and his goal scorin',
Ryan savin'
and boot blastin',
Bristow's ball winnin'
and passin'
Wills free kick winnin'
and chestin' in,
Stefan's slide tacklin'
and subin' on and off,
Morgan's dribblin'
and brilliant passin',
Rickson's ball stoppin'
and kickin',
Gardner's smackin'
and clearin' of the line.
That is Mordiford
football team.

Ashley Holmes (10)
Mordiford CE Primary School, Mordiford

My Dino

My dino is eight,
He tries to eat my mate.
He goes out on a date
And always comes home late.
Veggies, that's what he hates
And when he was nine
He ate all my mates
For a lovely dine!
I told him to go to bed
But he just bit off my head!

Charlie Hodges (10)
Mordiford CE Primary School, Mordiford

The River Life

I'm turquoise sheets with blue,
My river animals will swim with you.
I will be floaty if you are too,
The river life with green and blue.

Flowers flow along my banks, twirling.
The birds sweep across my banks, stirring.
The river is a wonderful life
When you're whirling.

Dreams and wishes drift like shadows in spring,
Lily pads float like a wedding ring.
The river life sounds like a flapping wing.

The river is alive.
The river is magical.
Twinkling stars are alight at night,
Now the river will say goodnight.

Alison Gardner (9)
Mordiford CE Primary School, Mordiford

The Magnificent Cat

My cat is black like the dark, night sky,
With the moon and stars on his side,
Like a witch's cat on a broomstick,
Sharp teeth like a crocodile eating his prey.

My cat will play with me,
Lively, running at the speed of light,
Hunting us down
Like a fox pouncing out.

Sleeping like an unknown object,
In a shadowy cave,
Like a dragon
In a deep slumber.

Joshua Carr (8)
Newton Burgoland School, Newton Burgoland

My Dog Poppy

My dog Poppy likes to run around,
Digging little holes, to see what she has found,
Poppy running back to us, with her ears out like a plane,
Mum will go mad, she's dirty again.

Poppy now has to go in the bath,
Put the shampoo on and scrub her down,
Watch the dirt go down the drain,
Now she is as clean as she used to be.

Poppy jumping to the towel, now she is nice and clean,
Her nose is shiny like leather again,
Her spots are black and white; her tongue is turning slimy,
She is rolling on the carpet, trying to get drier.

Mum is shouting, louder and louder,
Come back Poppy,
We don't want to do it again
Or else I'm sure we will be *insane!*

Jack Evans (9)
Newton Burgoland School, Newton Burgoland

Spooky Night

S tars twinkling in the bright sky,
P eople waiting for their goodnight scare,
O utside the witches are waiting.
O oh ahhhh! A haunted house with rats and bats,
K eep a watch on the ghosts inside!
Y es! We are in a haunted house.

N o one setting foot in the scary graveyard,
I magining you hear howling wolves getting closer.
G hosts and ghouls call out goodnight.
H eadless horsemen ride off into the night.
T he scare is over!

Abigail Williamson (7)
Newton Burgoland School, Newton Burgoland

My Dog

My dog likes to bark and play,
Nearly all night and all the day.

In the morning she never gets up,
She looks like a baby all curled up.

It's so peaceful now and quiet,
Until she wakes up and creates a big riot.

I run in the room and shout, 'It's okay, it's okay.'
But she never listens to me anyway.

I start to play a song on the piano,
The song I'm playing is called, 'O Leano'.

I don't think this helped Molly to sleep
Because I heard her starting to weep.

'I think I'm getting tired,' I said,
So we both went up to bed.

As soon as I lay down my head
She snuggled up on my bed.

Laura Coleman (10)
Newton Burgoland School, Newton Burgoland

The Magnificent Cheetah

My magnificent cheetah has spots like a white Dalmatian,
His teeth are like saws chopping down a tree,
Coming down to meet his death.
His prey runs away with the cheetah running after it,
Like a hunter catching his food with a big gun,
And then, *bang! Bang!*
The two animals are dead like the dinosaurs.

Drew Fores (8)
Newton Burgoland School, Newton Burgoland

Holly

Look!
Holly's ears flapping to and fro,
Her tail wagging like a helicopter's wing,
Her legs running like a cheetah's,
Here comes Holly!

Listen!
Holly munching, crunch, crunch on her food,
Crying at the door 'let me in' on her own,
Her panting, faster and faster, after her run,
Here comes Holly!

Feel!
Holly's silky coat of fur,
Her nose, like a piece of leather,
Her sharp teeth scratching on your leg,
Here comes Holly!

Nicholas Robinson (7)
Newton Burgoland School, Newton Burgoland

My Family

M um, Dad, Gurveena and Amman are my family.
Y awning, sleeping, dancing, that's my family.

F irst comes Mum, here comes Dad and right behind is us,
   they are my family.
A mman, quite mad, Gurveena, an angel, that's my family.
M adness is everywhere, that's my family.
I ntelligent and important, that's my family.
L oving, caring for each other, that's my family.
Y es! That's my family.

Rameeka Banning (9)
Newton Burgoland School, Newton Burgoland

Bad Table Manners

B ad table manners are very rude.
A ll people do is slurp and burp.
D ads telling their children off.

T able manners should be good, he says.
A rguing with your brother.
B ad manners - flicking peas, attacking cheese.
L ittle boys, little girls
E ating very noisily.

M eat and vegetables pushed around.
A piece of meat on the ground.
N aughty children, chewing with their mouths wide open.
N eglected food under the table.
E ating can be bad or good.
R udely or nicely, you can choose.
S ome people are well mannered and some quite rude.

Tom Evans (10)
Newton Burgoland School, Newton Burgoland

My Mother's Motorbike

M y mother's motorbike is small,
O ther motorbikes are slower.
T his motorbike is shiny.
O ver the ramps the motorbike goes,
R acing the people in cars down the free road.
B eing the fastest bike on the road,
I ncredible motorbike, it really is.
K eeps on going in all weathers,
E veryone sees mum in her leathers.

Jack Spencer (7)
Newton Burgoland School, Newton Burgoland

RSPCA Helps Animals

R escuing stray animals
S aving all their lives
P eople come and look at all the
C ats and dogs
A nimals are getting well at -

H armsworth Hospital in London
E very pet has some health problem
L etting owners know how much medicine to give their
P oorly pets
S o they'll soon be back to normal.

A nimals are found
N eglected by their owners
I n the middle of the night
M any people are asleep
A nimals ambulances drive around
L ondon's streets
S earching for animals, animals in distress.

Hannah Robinson (11)
Newton Burgoland School, Newton Burgoland

Colours Of The Rainbow

Red flames - of a bonfire
Orange clouds - when the sun is setting
Yellow daffodils - waving in the wind
Green grass - growing in the farmers' fields
Blue dolphins - splashing in the tumbling sea
Indigo sky - on a clear, frosty night
Violets - smell sweet, deep in the forest.

Daniel Glithero (10)
Newton Burgoland School, Newton Burgoland

My Dog Bilbo

Bilbo, he's lively, cheeky and crazy
But sometimes he can be rather lazy.

At night he curls up on his warm rug,
All snug and still then I'll give him a big hug.

He likes a long walk
And waiting for the ball.
He runs far down the field,
Then he bumps into another dog.
They sniff around, Bilbo walks off whining,
All sad and slow.

He loves his tricks and showing off.
He'll jump up and grab a fly or a moth.

But he's mine all mine!

Amelia McCausland (10)
Newton Burgoland School, Newton Burgoland

My Pets

After years of wanting a fish,
Here's one sitting in my dining room,
Swimming lazily around the tank.
I've got it - let's call it Sparky.

Poor old Sparky,
All his scales sticking out,
All white - poor Sparky,
The next day poor old Sparky was dead.

I've got another pet now,
It's cuddly, wriggly and bristly,
Its teeth are spiky, its eyes are beady,
It's a hamster called Disney.

Bethan Jacka (9)
Newton Burgoland School, Newton Burgoland

Dolphins

Dolphins are kind
Very cheerful indeed
They save us from danger
In the deep blue sea
They are the cutest creatures on Earth
They are lovable and blue
You can swim with them too
In a warm pool
But the saddest thing is
They get caught in the nets
Of fishermen catching tuna.

Sarah Davies (10)
Newton Burgoland School, Newton Burgoland

Untitled

Colonel Fabtastik Butterwork Toast,
Bought a mansion haunted by a ghost,
But the estate agent sat on his chair,
Forgot to mention the spectre was there.

Before the Colonel went in to dine,
He looked at the chimney and saw a sudden shine,
From out of the sooty thing came the awful ghost,
'Oh . . . are you the host?'

Little did the Colonel know,
That the old ghost was about to put on a little show,
The spectre rattled his chains and did bellow,
'This is my house, get out, you fellow!'

First class! Bravo!
But the ghost walked through a table too low,
The ghost got annoyed and floated away,
To go to another house to stay.

Andrew Ward (11)
Pinfold Street JMI School, Darlaston

Foxes Lurk

Foxes lurk within the grass
Never knowing where they'll end up,
They bound over fences,
Sneak and creep downstairs in our grass,
They'll get their prey by the end of the night,
Rabbits, hares or hedgehogs . . .
That's right!

Foxes - with orange coats.

Serena Sansara (9)
Pinfold Street JMI School, Darlaston

Snails

One day I walked up my path,
Where I noticed a slimy trail.
I followed it down the road,
Where I found a little snail.

His shell was shining bright,
His eyes were popping out.
He got tired very quickly,
As he slid slowly about.

Kara Page (10)
Pinfold Street JMI School, Darlaston

Homework

Homework buzzes around on paper
Then creeps up into your brain
Makes your head go all bumpy
And then end up in pain.

Emma Rollason (10)
Pinfold Street JMI School, Darlaston

Spiders

Spiders are horrid
They go up your nose.
They hide in your favourite place
And even in a rose.

Spiders are evil
They do a nasty pose.
Then they go for the kill
When your eyes close.

Akaash Ram (9)
Pinfold Street JMI School, Darlaston

Cat Ripper

Floor smeller
Cat ripper
Ball catcher
Bell attached
Stalks all day
Hawk eyes
Fast runner
Animal stunner.
What am I?

Sam Orchard (11)
Portleven School, Portleven

Summer On Beaches

Summer on beaches
With ice creams and shiny sun
Swimming in the sea
With rubber rings on the beach
And building sandcastles, *fun!*

Paris Penhaligon (11)
Portleven School, Portleven

Nonsense Meadow

A beautiful scene
Of blue and green
If you carefully look
You'll see a babbling brook
This is really too sensible
The words are not free to run and ddrriiiibbbbllle.

This is more like it
A meadow is like a great armpit
With cheesy cheeps of bonkers birds
And carnivorous cows in endless herds
Where beautiful butterflies fight
Even piranhas do not bite.

This meadow is neither nonsense
Or completely plain sense
The meadow is a wondrous mad land
Even though most of it is sand
None who enters exits alive
Although in this place animals thrive.

Carl Betts (10)
Portleven School, Portleven

What Am I?

Squeaky voice,
Trouble maker,
Cheese snatcher,
Naughty nibbler,
Silky coat,
Long windy tail,
Tiny teeth that never fail,
Beady eyes,
Big fat grin,
I'm cute altogether.

What am I?

A mouse!

Zoe Davies (11)
Portleven School, Portleven

The Hokey-Pokey Swamp

In the Hokey-Pokey swamp,
Lived the Hokey-Pokey monster.
With his Hokey-Pokey teeth,
He'll poke you if he wants to.

In the Hokey-Pokey swamp,
Lived the Hokey-Pokey shark,
And on the Hokey-Pokey trees,
He eats all the bark.

In the Hokey-Pokey swamp,
Lived the Hokey-Pokey people.
Don't disturb them,
'Cause they're pretty lethal.

The Hokey-Pokey wife,
With her Hokey-Pokey knife
And the Hokey-Pokey man,
With his Hokey-Pokey clan.

Jowan Shanberg (10)
Portleven School, Portleven

Seasons

Shiny spring
When lambs are born
Looking around all forlorn.

Sparkling summer
Time for holidays
School is over, time to play.

Amazing autumn
Leaves they fall
Time for kids to go to school.

Wicked winter
Snowy days
The year is over with freezing days.

Gemma Harding (10)
Portleven School, Portleven

Spellin' Chek

I cant spall spell
I cant wite write right
My spellin iss gobley-goop
From the hookey-pookey well.

I cant tipe type
I cant doodle-doodle right
Me spellin is lick an ifant
From Mrs janes joones johns jones class.

I cant prink print
I cant paant paint
I'm wers than an ifant
I'm like wot I am lake.

I'm like a 10, 9, 8, 7, 6, 5, 4, 3, 2, 1 yer old
From the hooli-kooli swamp
I'm wubis, I cant spall spell, wite write right
Tipe type, doodle-doodle rigt, pwint print
Paant paint.

I just cant spall.

Will Dawson (11)
Portleven School, Portleven

Winter

W inter is a cold season
 I n the year of 2004
N ow it is raining
T he hail is on its way
E njoy the winter
R eally I do as long as I do not get too cold.

Kerensa Lewis (11)
Portleven School, Portleven

I Will Dream About . . .

I will dream about . . .
A feather from an Emu flying in the air
A windy day in a poppy field
And monkeys swinging from tree to tree in the jungle.

I will dream about . . .
Being in the North Pole with penguins and polar bears
Washing machines going around and around
Like the Earth spinning on its axis
And the first word of a newborn baby.

I will dream about . . .
A massive mountain in India
A newly born lamb with its proud mother
And walking on water with weird water walking boots.

I will dream about . . .
Golden leaves falling off trees
A blind man relying on his guide dog as his best friend
And a cold, snowy day with everyone building snowmen.

I will dream about . . .
Being in my bed with a friendly, furry bedspread
With a magic chocolate pillow
And cuddle a soft, shiny, silver, silky teddy.

I will dream about . . .
A new life 'down under'
With scorching sun, sea and sand
And snorkelling under the water, watching wonderful fish swim by.

Katie Evans (11)
Portleven School, Portleven

Seasons

In the summertime
People like to have a drink of wine
They sit in the pub
Eating all the grub
They walk round the harbour
And meet John Barber
That's what I love about summer.

In the wintertime
You don't drink as much wine
Santa leaves the presents out
All in a pile, all in a mount
And then he eats his mince pie
Before he rides back into the sky
That's what I love about winter.

In the autumn time
Nobody drinks any wine
All the leaves fall off the trees
And not much honey for the bees
I like to collect all the conkers
Before you go really bonkers
That's what I love about autumn.

In the springtime
Everyone drinks lots of wine
All the flowers begin to bloom
You can even smell the spring perfume
It is the season of flora day
Hip hip hip hooray
The birds come out to play
That's what I love about spring.

Lamorna Newman (9)
Portleven School, Portleven

Public Toilets

Full to bursting,
I feel all loose,
I wish I hadn't drunk so much
Orange juice.

What a long queue,
I don't know if I can make it
My record for holding on is 10 seconds
Let's see if I can break it . . .

Aaah! Relief!

I don't feel so bad now,
I've done what I wanted to do,
My leg has gone all warm,
And there's squelching in my shoe.

David Ferris (11)
Portleven School, Portleven

Fireworks

Remember, remember the 5th of November,
On Guy Fawkes night fireworks are bright.
Bright coloured showers exploding in the dark sky,
Fireworks jumping high into the velvety darkness.
Children parading with Guy Fawkes on sticks,
Children wearing glowing crowns.
The next event is Christmas time,
But the next day it's all just a blur.

Evie Hayman (10)
Portleven School, Portleven

Night Mail Trains

This is the train putting letters in its pockets,
This is the children eating their lockets,
This is you lying on the floor,
Never hearing the knock on the door,
Sending letters to people with flu,
Sending letters to people on a canoe,
Sending letters from the Royal Mail,
But the letters never fail,
To make your door.
At night the train goes past your house,
When you're asleep it is as quiet as a mouse,
At the end the train goes home,
Just a dog running after his bone,
In the night he is very tired,
But you never know, it might get fired.

Josh Shepherd (10)
St Martin's CE Primary School, Bilston

Funny Face Peter

There was a man named
Funny Face Peter,
Who ate an extra large
Pizza,
He gobbled it down,
Like a big clown!
Then he decreased
To less than a
Metre!

Louis Pullen & Adam Stokes (11)
St Martin's CE Primary School, Bilston

What Is Pink?

Pink is bright with a colourful crayon,
Pink is some nice fizzy pop.
Pink is for a king who wears a cloak,
Pink is a cotton wool pencil case.

Pink is a pen that is nice and bright,
Pink is for a fat, chunky pig,
Pink is for a tall flamingo in the water,
Pink is when people dye their hair.

Pink is a footballer when he plays football,
Pink is for a girl wearing a pink, beautiful bobble,
Pink is a vest that people wear,
Pink is a mansion in the middle of nowhere.

Pink is everything!

Mitchell Pearson (10)
St Martin's CE Primary School, Bilston

What Am I?

I fly in the night sky
I hunt and make them die
I am blind but I can still catch them
I can smell them from a mile away
I eat mice and worms if I'm a beginner
I catch them for my dinner
I come out at night
I sleep in the light.

What am I?

A: An owl

Toni James (11)
St Martin's CE Primary School, Bilston

The Monkey

The monkey lives in a zoo
He eats lots of bananas too
And more sultanas
He's very, very cheeky
He swings from tree to tree
His name is Lee
He's always climbing a tree
He's always getting into mischief.

He's always making people laugh
He is very cunning
He is very hairy
He's got lots of friends - one is Mary
She's hairy and very scary.

Kirsty Brown (10)
St Martin's CE Primary School, Bilston

Mouth

A good-gobbler
A wide-opener
A constant-eater
A yawn-helper
A noise-bringer
A finger-sucker
A lip-clicker
A loud-shouter
A sharp-whistler
A gob-stopper!

Natasha Laithwaite (10)
St Martin's CE Primary School, Bilston

Haunted House

The windows are so dirty they look like they haven't been washed.
The roof is ragged, so ragged it could fall off.
The haunted house is creepy,
It has a spell that makes you sleepy.
It has vampires and ghosts, all wicked things,
Some of them have wings.
There are cobwebs in the windows,
Also spiders in there.
It's so hot it's like a sauna.
Some rooms are cold, so cold you could freeze.
There are things that make you sneeze.
It is as dark as a vampire's cape
But they don't let you escape.
So watch out, don't go in there.
If you do, good luck but beware!

Shannon Edwards (8)
St Martin's CE Primary School, Bilston

What Am I?

I live in the water,
I am big and blue,
I eat small things,
I am bigger than you!

I make crying noises,
I make a move,
A jump above the water,
I do a big splash!

What am I?

Lauren Jackson (11)
St Martin's CE Primary School, Bilston

I Am . . . ?

I slither about the ground and trees,
I creep around your knees.
I sometimes have venom,
I am a predator,
I eat fleshy creatures, plump and juicy,
I live in forests and hot places.

What am I?

Jamie Guest (11)
St Martin's CE Primary School, Bilston

The Snow

The snow is like a cold ice cream
Dropped from its ice cream cone!
The snow is like a white blanket
Being spread over the ground.
The snow is a big ice cube
Sliding from its tray.
The snow is a fluffy cotton ball
From a cotton cloud.

Kai Sadler (11)
St Martin's CE Primary School, Bilston

Dog

Fast-runner,
tail-wagger,
eye-beamer,
nose-twitcher,
claw-scratcher,
tongue-dribbler.

Billy Henderson (10)
St Martin's CE Primary School, Bilston

Smile

Smile, go on, smile!
Anyone would think to look at you
That your cat is on a barbecue!

If you don't you will look like a man
That has been run over by a van!

Just smile
Unless you want to run a mile.
Go on, smile!

Wayne Lees (11)
St Martin's CE Primary School, Bilston

Mother

M is for making you feel like you're flying.
O is for obedience which all mothers have.
T is for terrific times together.
H is for happiness which she always brings.
E is for every day to be special.
R is for the respect that she gives.

Gemma Green (11)
St Martin's CE Primary School, Bilston

Wizard's Den

The wizard's den doesn't have a door
And when you go in there is no way out.
There is no fresh air in a wizard's den.
It is dark in a wizard's den and very hard to see.
Just be careful if you walk into a wizard's den.
You can only run.

Curtis Nicholls
St Martin's CE Primary School, Bilston

Bullies

Bullies, bullies, what's the attraction?
Power, glory, piece of the action?
Well, let me just say you're not so tough
to pick on the weak it's really quite rough!

The damage, the pain that bullying can do
leave scars and hurt all down to you.
Think how you would feel in their shoes
crying and sad, suffering the blues!

Bullying is bad, bullying is cruel.
Do you think it makes you rule?
It doesn't, you know, it makes you bad
but most of all it makes you sad.

One day you'll grow up with kids of your own.
How will you feel when they get home
and you will ask what happened today?
'I got punched in the face and ran away!'

You'll feel sad for yourself
and your kids too
because you'll know that once
that bully was you!

Jemma Mansell (10)
St Martin's CE Primary School, Bilston

Mouse

My cousin, who is bossy, is named Kelly
Has got a cute dog called Ellie
And Kelly was playing with Billy
But he was being silly
Then they went to Kelly's house
And they saw a mouse
And then they went to the shop
To buy some pop
And then they went back to Kelly's house
And there was no mouse.

Leanne Tanner (10)
St Martin's CE Primary School, Bilston

Dogs

I love dogs.
Dogs are sweet,
I need them
So I can live.

I love dogs.
They have to drink,
They need a home
So they can live.

I love them.
My dog loves me,
He drinks water
And something for tea.

They play with each other.
They usually bark.
My dog plays with me,
So dogs will play with you in the park.

Shannon Salter (9)
St Martin's CE Primary School, Bilston

Pussy Cat

Here is a cat
Cutting its paw,
Crossing a station
And banging a door.

Eating its dinner
He doesn't get thinner,
Shouting at its mummy
And shaking its tummy.

Running from a dog
Chasing a hog,
Running upstairs
And flicking his hairs.

Aaron Asprey (9)
St Martin's CE Primary School, Bilston

In Space

Maybe in space
There's a red planet Mars,
A giant, smelly monster,
And brightly coloured stars.

Maybe in space
There's planets big and small,
Aliens low and tall,
And seas floating smoothly.

Maybe in space
There's cheesy-coloured moons dancing,
Huge spaceships singing and prancing,
And the blue sky wobbling and shaking.

Maybe in space
There's magical yellow suns sparkling,
And everything else shining
And smiling happily.

Maybe in space
There's fights and wars,
Lots of broken laws,
And planets who are unhappy with falling shores.

Maybe an alien would come up to you,
Maybe even poke you too,
He might even give you some advice,
But if you're lucky not the lice.

He'd say,
This is space,
Not your place,
Go on, shove off.

Go on, get lost,
I'll send you all my bad things,
Nothing like diamonds, rubies and rings,
We don't need you, so shoo, shoo, shoo!

Don't push me, I'm old and smelly,
That was the end of that space,
And now I'm off to my place.
Bye!

Paige Strong (10)
St Martin's CE Primary School, Bilston

The Express Train

Can you see the express train?
Just like people using their brain.
As you go by the towers,
Sometimes you can smell fresh flowers.
Like you see the poor,
Knocking on people's doors.

As you see swimming pools,
Sometimes you drive past schools.
When you see rivers,
Sometimes you see people having shivers.

As you cross the border,
Giving people orders,
Asleep in Edinburgh,
Awake in boring Glasgow
Just down in Aberdeen.

Some people are boring
And some people can be boring.
When you see cars.
Sometimes you can say ta-tas.

As you see their speed,
Like you take the lead.
We get on the train,
Then we get off again.
Now it's time to go home.

Aaron Modi (9)
St Martin's CE Primary School, Bilston

The Witch's Kitchen

There was a scuttling mouse
When I went in the house
I went in the kitchen
And a saw a big pot
To put people in
I heard someone creaking down the stairs
I saw a witch wearing a crown
I sneaked up to have a little peek.

Jade Alder (9)
St Martin's CE Primary School, Bilston

School Life

In the beginning it was just fun.
Playing all day long, life had just begun.

Then came Year 1, the shock of our lives,
English, science and counting in fives.

Next came Year 2 and to our dismay,
SATstests were the order of the day.

In our fourth year (that means Year 3)
We did even more maths and literacy.

After that came Year 4 and it was quite cool.
We started swimming at the local pool.

Year 5 was the best, you can't deny.
With fun things to do, the year just flew by.

Now we're in Year 6, the worst year of all,
With never-ending tests, it's like a brick wall.

But I really enjoyed it (apart from the test!)
I really like our school, I think it's the best!

Hannah Compton (11)
Sutton-in-Craven CP School, Keighley

He

He sits there in the corner,
weeping all day through,
and everybody in the classroom,
they don't know what to do.

The tears roll down his soft, red face,
and onto the stony floor,
and he thought of the smiling faces,
and the joy which was no more.

He watched the birds pass by,
they chirped and dipped through the clouds,
and spiralled round in a circle,
and twisted through the white shrouds.

And he said to himself, 'Why,
why do the birds fly in the sky?
How can they twist and turn
and how do they soar so very high?'

And the bell rang through the hall,
he walked down the twisty road
and through the shrubs and trees
and on the floor was a toad.

'Why, why can't everything live forever
instead of having to die
and why do I keep on wondering
why, why, why?'

Callum Thomas (10)
Sutton-in-Craven CP School, Keighley

Teach Us

Teachers seem to be really good
But underneath they're just like us.
They're naughty, sneaky
And even cheeky.
When they come to school and we're not there
They play nasty tricks
And stick chewing gum on our chair.

They don't teach us anything at all
Because their brains are so small
And head teachers are the worst of all,
Their office is such a tip.
They hide wine in their drawers.
All the teachers do more shouting than they do teaching.
They should all be fired, those little liars.
Aaaaaahhhhh! Quick, stop writing, the teacher's coming!

Shannon Cassidy & Naomi Tennant (11)
Sutton-in-Craven CP School, Keighley

Holding The Baby

They said they'd let me hold her
on the settee at home.
I sat on the settee, my feet in the air,
excited but worried she might fall.
I looked down at her, I could see her veins
and her little, yellow, spotty face.
She was cuddly and soft and very cute and chubby,
just like a baby should be!
I stroked her head, with little, soft hairs,
I heard mum saying, 'Don't drop her.'

It was like she was a new kitten
but she's grown up now like a cat.

Esther Liu (8)
Sutton-in-Craven CP School, Keighley

The Hare And The Tortoise

One day the hare was making fun
of a tortoise who was slow.
The hare said loudly, 'I can run
and you can't even go!'

The hare demanded to run a race,
the tortoise agreed to it.
So they would run at great, fast pace,
the hare ran in his kit.

The hare started off running fast,
the tortoise came along.
The hare was dashing very fast,
the tortoise took so long.

The hare lazily fell asleep,
so the tortoise he crept past.
The hare he gave a quick peep
and quickly jumped up and dashed.

The tortoise quickly went on to win,
the hare came jumping along.
The tortoise was running king,
hare really did think wrong.

Emma Lang (9) & Rosie Bonser (10)
Sutton-in-Craven CP School, Keighley

Winter

W ind in my face
I am cold
N ear a shelter I feel safe
T in cans blow about
E yes are red
R ain is falling.

Benjamin Fletcher (9)
Sutton-in-Craven CP School, Keighley

The Hare And The Tortoise

One day the hare was making fun
of a tortoise who was slow.
The hare said loudly, 'I can run
and you can't even go!'

The tortoise he was very cross,
he said, 'Let's have a race.'
Hare thought proudly he was the boss
and was happy to join the chase.

A passing fox set off the race,
he yelled, 'Ready, steady, go!'
The hare rushed off at such a fast pace
but tortoise went very slow.

The hare stopped off for a little rest,
tortoise slowly crept past.
The hare still thought he was the best
then he found out he was last.

Rebecca Brown (10)
Sutton-in-Craven CP School, Keighley

Winter

The snow is falling on the ground,
As quiet as a mouse, making no sound,
Making a white carpet on the lawn,
It will be covered with footprints by dawn.
It is untouched but not for long,
Just until the children come.
Animals rush for cover; rabbits, they hide low
But the children go *crunch*, *crunch* in the soft white snow.
Children shout, scream with delight,
Making a snowman with all their might.
They love to roar, bellow and prance.
They sing, have sledge rides and, best of all, they dance.

Catherine Walker (10)
Sutton-in-Craven CP School, Keighley

The Boy Who Cried Wolf

A rainy day a boy was told to stay
With a flock of boring sheep.
He decided to go and play
But the rain was so deep.

The boy cried as loud as he could,
'Wolf, wolf,' to his friends.
People came running as fast as they could,
The sheep ran to their pens.

He did it a couple of times,
The boy was laughing like mad.
Again people came running in lines,
He knew he was being bad.

A wolf was prowling nearby
But the wolf could not be seen.
The boy saw the wolf and gave a great cry,
He wished he had come clean.

Not one person would believe him,
No one would come to help.
He realised lying was a sin
And should learn when to yelp!

Kaya Whitehead (10)
Sutton-in-Craven CP School, Keighley

A Bat Biter

A night sneaker
A blood sucker
A night screecher
A night stalker
A night biter
A night flyer.

Ashley Colman (10)
Sutton-in-Craven CP School, Keighley

The Hare And The Tortoise

One day a hare was making fun
of a tortoise who was slow.
The hare said loudly, 'You can't run
and I am ready to go.'

The hare challenged tortoise to a race,
tortoise said, 'Alright, I can.'
The hare set off with lots of pace
while tortoise made a plan.

Hare stopped off for a little rest
while tortoise came plodding past.
Tortoise won, he was the best
and hare came trailing last.

Hare said, 'Well done, it was fine
plus it was lots of fun!'
Tortoise said, 'The pleasure is mine,'
and they were glad it was done.

Adam Birks (10)
Sutton-in-Craven CP School, Keighley

Night At School - Haiku

The dark, silent hall,
Blowing leaves on the playground,
Shadows in the class.

Daniel Kirk (10)
Sutton-in-Craven CP School, Keighley

T-Rex

A big, fat monster
A long-ago carnivore
A frightening being
A very small, minute brain.

Aaron Tattersall-Jarvis (10)
Sutton-in-Craven CP School, Keighley

Summer

This is our place
The trees are strong with lots of branches
And all the leaves have started to sprout

The river is flowing slowly
And the breeze is lovely to hear
As I know summer is here
Because the sun is steaming hot.

Everything is wonderful
Because the trees are strong,
The leaves are sprouting,
The river is flowing silently and slowly
So everything is fine.

Amelia McManus (8)
Sutton-in-Craven CP School, Keighley

Ghost!

A midnight scarer
A door unlocker
A window creeper
A mighty glider
A midnight walker.

Ahhhhh!

Christopher Town (10)
Sutton-in-Craven CP School, Keighley

Shadows

A quiet creeper
A dark darer
A mean mover
A sleeping waker
A night watcher.

Holly Greenwood (10)
Sutton-in-Craven CP School, Keighley

Winter Is . . .

Winter is a time to let an icicle make a smile on your face.
The sprinkle of an icy piece of lace
But you watch out,
The sun will appear in no time
And you will sing a cheerful rhyme.
Then the sun will come once more,
Then the cold will appear once more
But then you will wake up and say
I saw the sun
But now it's back to boring cold.

Sarah Winter (9)
Sutton-in-Craven CP School, Keighley

Christmas Is . . .

Christmas is red and sparkly like Santa's coat.
It tastes like the huge Christmas turkey with gravy.
It smells like roast potatoes boiling in a pan.
It looks like children playing in soft, white snow.
It sounds like little robin redbreast singing sweetly.
It feels like it's cosy and warm like a nice cup of hot chocolate.

Jacob Uren (9)
Sutton-in-Craven CP School, Keighley

Anger

Anger is black like a storming bull,
It tastes like boiling, over-cooked burgers,
It smells like petrol wetting the floor,
It looks like a hotel's ashes sprinkled on the ground,
It sounds like the screeching of brakes,
It feels like a dead body on fire.

Thomas Mortimer (9)
Sutton-in-Craven CP School, Keighley

Laughs

Laughs are always here,
Laughs are always there,
A laugh is joyful,
Laughs always care!

Laughs are popular,
Laughs are fun
And are as sweet as a chocolate bun!

So, all that I can say about laughs,
Is that they are better than maths!

Katy Lloyd (10)
Sutton-in-Craven CP School, Keighley

Christmas Is . . .

Christmas is white like sparkly snow on the frosty ground.
It tastes like crunchy bacon wrapped around sausages.
It smells like Christmas dinner out on the table.
It looks like the wintry snow coming from the sky.
It feels like the warmness from our turkey.

Bethany Wild (9)
Sutton-in-Craven CP School, Keighley

Christmas Is . . .

Christmas is gold like a pirate's treasure.
It smells like custard bubbling in the pan.
It tastes like a warm turkey dinner.
It looks like a room full of presents.
It sounds like children playing and laughing.
It feels like chocolate melting on my tongue.

Johnathan Wilkinson (10)
Sutton-in-Craven CP School, Keighley

Friends

If no one had friends
What would life be like?
Standing alone in the playground
Or riding alone on your bike.

Some people in the world
Have no friends at all,
Just sitting alone all day
And not getting a phone call.

Me, I'm lucky,
I am lots of fun,
So don't just sit and be miserable
Remember; fun lasts when you're young!

Emily Edgar (11)
Sutton-in-Craven CP School, Keighley

Icy Days

W inter makes the grass frosty
 I cy, white snow covering the floor.
N ew gloves, scarves, hats.
T ins blowing about frantically.
E ye-catching *icicles*.
R un outside at ten past ten.

Oliver Robertshaw (9)
Sutton-in-Craven CP School, Keighley

Winter

W hite snow falls on the ground.
 I n the park people make snowmen.
N ature is hibernating in warm places.
T he robins are sitting in the trees.
E veryone is sledging in the snow.
R eindeer run round and round.

Fern Worsencroft (9)
Sutton-in-Craven CP School, Keighley

Dream Of This Horse

Horses gallop about so fast,
Gently prancing all over the grass,
It doesn't matter if mare or foal,
At least they are much better than a mole.

Look at the jumps they jump at the show,
Padding along the white, fresh snow,
They go flying over the jumps so quick,
At the end of the day they deserve a lick.

Is this a dream or is this true?
I think this is true, so do you,
Dream, dream, dream of a horse,
Some day the dream will come true of course.

Ella Beaumont (10)
Sutton-in-Craven CP School, Keighley

A Dog Called Freddy

There once was a dog called Freddy,
That had a very big beddy.
Strange cos he's small
And not very tall,
That strange little dog named Freddy.

Georgina Robinson (11)
Sutton-in-Craven CP School, Keighley

Love

Love looks like happiness,
Love tastes like sweets,
Love sounds like laughter,
Love smells like strawberries,
Love feels really warm.

Alex Blackie (10)
Sutton-in-Craven CP School, Keighley

Friends

Friends are there to give a helping hand,
Friends are there to always understand.

Friends will be there no matter what,
They'd even tell you if you had a spot.

Friends are forever,
They stay together.

A friend will give all they can give,
Without a friend there's no reason to live.

Rebecca Dunwell (11)
Sutton-in-Craven CP School, Keighley

Ghost!

A midnight stalker
An air glider
A landing creeper
A door creaker
A curtain mover
A graveyard waker.
Ahhhhh!

Sian Butler (11)
Sutton-in-Craven CP School, Keighley

Pip

Pip is . . .
A proud prowler
A mouse catcher
A furry feline
An unpredictable pouncer
Pip is a wonderful cat.

Stacey Dwyer (10)
Sutton-in-Craven CP School, Keighley

My Gran

My gran is as cuddly as a bear.
Her hair is like tangled wire.
Her eyes are like the big blue sea.
Her face is like a crinkled bag.
When she walks she is like a striding lion.
When she sits she is like a ball.
When she laughs she is like a parrot.
When she sleeps she is like a baby.
The best thing about my gran is that she cares for me.

Joseph Buffey (8)
Sutton-in-Craven CP School, Keighley

A Zombie Stalker

A night creeper
A night stalker
A night walker
A night sneaker
A night seeker
A bloodsucker
A night biter
A night frightener.

Alessandro De Vito (10)
Sutton-in-Craven CP School, Keighley

Volcano

A loud banger
A fiery mountain
A big smoker
A country destroyer.

Louise Marratt (11)
Sutton-in-Craven CP School, Keighley

Winter

W inter is cold and slippery
I ce, it stiffens the river
N ice is winter, it is good for playing in
T he snow, it makes me go brrrr
E veryone loves winter, it's because it's cold
R ivers, you can go ice-skating on.

We love winter!

Becky Simpson (9)
Sutton-in-Craven CP School, Keighley

Winter

W hite snow all around
I n all types of woollen clothes
N o sun to be seen
T he trees are bare everywhere
E very day is very cold with icicles and snow
R un inside, get warm, not outside to be cold.

Adam Stares (9)
Sutton-in-Craven CP School, Keighley

Twister

A roof taker
A car catcher
A spinning saucer
A sucking vacuum
A building terroriser.

What am I?

Jude McManus (11)
Sutton-in-Craven CP School, Keighley

Winter

W hite snow is coming from the skies
and the bugs are saying their goodbyes.
I n the house it's breaking dawn
and on the other side it's warm.
N o more things around
and everything is hard like the ground.
T oday all the snow is there
and everyone is here.
E veryone not inside
but outside.
R ain is coming from the skies
and snow is saying its goodbyes.

Stephen Ettery (9)
Sutton-in-Craven CP School, Keighley

Summer

S ummer is the most beautiful thing.
U s playing in the street.
M oney lying in the street.
M an, it's so hot.
E verything is very, very hot.
R unning in the street.

Daniel Lovell (8)
Sutton-in-Craven CP School, Keighley

Bullies Haiku

They are so horrid
They're mean to the nice people
I hate all of them.

Angela Hayton (11)
Sutton-in-Craven CP School, Keighley

Winter

W hite snow drops to the ground
I bring snow all around
N ice snowmen will be built
T he snow and wind slaps my cheeks
E veryone helps me build a snowman
R un indoors when it gets too cold!

James Beaumont (8)
Sutton-in-Craven CP School, Keighley

In Sixty Years' Time

In sixty years' time,
I'll be sixty-nine.
On the TV,
I'll be watching Dragon Ball Z.

Cars will fly,
As I pass by.
I'll walk my dog each day,
And meet my friends on the way.

Josh Waller (8)
Sutton-in-Craven CP School, Keighley

Winter

W ild and windy
I n early and out early
N ights are shorter
T rees are bare
E xcitement is all around
R olling in the snow.

Harris Catley (9)
Sutton-in-Craven CP School, Keighley

Summer Place

This is our summer place
And the trees are full of brown branches
And all the leaves are bright green on the trees
And the river is running gently.
The air is warm from the hot sun,
Our voices talk clearly to each other
And everything is bright.

Ashley Hollings (8)
Sutton-in-Craven CP School, Keighley

Winter

W hite snow falls on the ground
I n the icy fields and on the grass
N obody hardly was going for a walk
T he road was full of ice and quiet
E ven the bulldogs were quiet, no barking, ice was covering
    the dogs
R ough winds blew through the farm.

Louise Grace Hinchcliffe (8)
Sutton-in-Craven CP School, Keighley

Winter

W ind is howling in the air
I cicles hanging from a cave
N ow we know that winter is here
T he children play happily in the snow
E verybody is wrapping up warm
R ain is seen once more.

Laura Feather (9)
Sutton-in-Craven CP School, Keighley

Weather

The crimson sun rises in the east,
the crimson sun sets in the west,
the crimson sun blows away the night,
all of the houses light up bright!

The beating rain comes from the sea,
the beating rain smashes down on me,
the beating rain can be fun
but the floods come by the ton!

The cold, cold snow is so white,
the cold, cold snow is so bright,
sit by the fire with some tea,
all of this warms up me!

The howling wind really does blow
and it will keep all the snow,
it is fine for flying kites,
get them up to very great heights!

Jake Cawthorne (9)
Sutton-in-Craven CP School, Keighley

My New Baby Cousin

I have a baby cousin.
Her name is Claire.
I play with her every day
But still she is very rare.

She plays in the cupboard.
She plays in the bed.
Claire is a little monster
And she always bangs her head.

Rachel Hargreaves (8)
Sutton-in-Craven CP School, Keighley

Winter

W e will sing carols
I ce is sparkling
N aughty children throw snow
T urkey we eat on Christmas Day
E very adult goes for a walk
R obins sing in winter.

Stefan Grant (8)
Sutton-in-Craven CP School, Keighley

Dolphins

D iving around in the sea
O ther people don't care for dolphins
L ittle dolphins to older dolphins
P layful in the water
H aving to be adopted so you can make them happy
I n the sea, blue everywhere
N othing can be cuter
S uch beautiful creatures.

Catherine Tupling (10)
Trinity Croft CE (A) J&I School, Rotherham

Army Weapons

If I was in the army, I would drive a tank
If I was in the army, I would shoot a Tommy gun
If I was in the army, I would fly a Spitfire plane
If I was in the army, I would be a bomb disposal man
If I was in the army, I would be an MP
If I was in the army, I would be off to war.

Alex Atkinson (10)
Trinity Croft CE (A) J&I School, Rotherham

The Weapon

The weapon is coming
The weapon of mass destruction
It's coming! It's coming!
Boom!

Am I the only survivor?
My town has gone!
I've got no family to go to!
Oh help!

Aaron Kirkby (9)
Trinity Croft CE (A) J&I School, Rotherham

Winter

Winter is cool
When children are not at school
When snowflakes fall and babies crawl
Winter is fun when adults run from snowballing kids
Winter is cool when Jack Frost comes out to play
Winter is hard
Skate on the ice
Hope it doesn't rain.

Danielle Booth (10)
Trinity Croft CE (A) J&I School, Rotherham

Pop Group Busted!

Singing rock songs
Jumpin' in the air
Wearing clothes so cool
Like rocking stars.

Kelly Schofield (10)
Trinity Croft CE (A) J&I School, Rotherham

Seasons

Summer is great, you can have fun
You can enjoy your summer as you laugh and run.

Winter is great, you can have fun,
Make snowmen, throw snowballs, sledge and run.

Autumn is great, you can have fun
As leaves fall around the ground, golden in the sun.

Spring is when the leaves grow, so you can have fun
Snowdrops and daffodils shine in the morning sun.

Dea Skidmore (11)
Trinity Croft CE (A) J&I School, Rotherham

The Robin

The robin perched silently
On the old, gnarled branch.
The robin's rosy, bright breast
Stands out to all nature.
Its soft, silky feathers
Keep it warm in the cold air.
Its sweet song rings around the frosty woods.
Its beady black eyes
Swivel round rapidly.

Harry Cowley (11)
Whitminster CE Primary School, Whitminster

The Robin

The robin has silky, soft, smooth feathers.
He has a glowing red chest.
His rotund body is perched on the window sill.
The robin has black beady eyes
Looking around for food.

Ryan Clark (9)
Whitminster CE Primary School, Whitminster

Chubby, Dumpy, Little Robin

Chubby, dumpy, little robin
Perched so high on a branch.

Chubby, dumpy, little robin
With your rocking, red, rosy breast.

Chubby, dumpy, little robin
Your shiny, silky, smooth feathers glittering as you eat red,
ripe berries.

Chubby, dumpy, little robin
We will see you in the cotton candy snow.

Chubby, dumpy, little robin
Keeping an eye on danger that passes by.

Chubby, dumpy, little robin
The bird we love at Christmas time.

Charlotte Parcel (10)
Whitminster CE Primary School, Whitminster

Sun!

Sun is a beautiful and bright person.
She makes me feel happy whenever she is around.
Her face looks like a big, blazing ball of fire.
Her eyes are always glistening like stars in the sky.
Her mouth is always smiling and cheerful.
Her hair is long and wavy.
She wears a long, silky dress
And a wreath of daisies around her head.
When she moves her hair sways side to side.
When she speaks the birds sing.
She lives in the clouds with the doves and angels.
Sun shines on me.

Victoria Thomas (10)
Whitminster CE Primary School, Whitminster

It's Winter

It's winter again!
The season for happiness and family.
The time for presents and giving.
The time for roasting hot fires and cups of hot tea.
It's winter again.

It's winter again!
The snow falls thick on the frosty ground.
Crunching and crackling under my feet.
It sparkles in the sun.

It's winter again!
The icy wind rips the leaves off the trees.
Makes you feel cold and horrible.
It's winter again.

Millie Lander (10)
Whitminster CE Primary School, Whitminster

Winter

Winter is a season of joy!
A season for skiing,
A season for crispy, white snow,
A season for glistening icicles,
A season for outdoor sports.

Winter is a season of sleep!
A season to hibernate,
A season to fly to other countries,
A season to sing.
Winter is a season so wonderful!

Nicolas Edwards (10)
Whitminster CE Primary School, Whitminster

Sun

Sun is a smiley, shining, fantastic girl.
She makes me feel warm, cosy and safe.
Her face looks like the colour of golden buttercups.
Her eyes dazzle in the bright, brilliant, morning light orange.
Her mouth is smiley, shimmering, glistening, blazing red.
Her hair is long and wavy, the colour of golden corn waving
in the field.
Her clothes are made of soft, slinky, silky, smooth silk.
When she moves she moves slowly but stylishly.
When she speaks the sound is like beautiful, brilliant birds
chirping on their branches.
She lives up high in the skylight sky on the clouds of Heaven.
Sun is a kind, cheery, beautiful girl to me!

Lorna Clague (10)
Whitminster CE Primary School, Whitminster

The Warrior Robin

Soaring through the sky like a lone warrior,
Your rosy red breast
A shield protecting you from the dangers all around.
Your beautiful voice alerting others to your presence,
Echoing around the world.
Your war against winter carries on forever,
Your only break between winter and autumn.
As you scavenge for food on tables up high,
Other birds, far superior, join you
But you do not run because you are a warrior.
You are a robin!

Kristian Cheshire (11)
Whitminster CE Primary School, Whitminster

The Robin

The robin is a small, dumpy bird,
Sitting on the window sill,
With a blood-red chest,
Singing all day long,
Searching for food,
In the ground or on the table,
Looking through its tiny, beady eyes.
The vibrant colours stand out from the white snow.
It swoops softly and silently
And the wings shine in the morning sun.
The robin is a winter bird.

Toby Gray (10)
Whitminster CE Primary School, Whitminster

Winter

The snow glitters and glistens on the snow-covered ground.
The icicles shimmer and sparkle as they hang off the rooftops
        of houses.
The lights on the tops of the houses twinkle and flash.
The frozen lakes shimmer and shine as the moonlight beams
        down on them.
The frost in the morning on the ground so slippery.
Sledging down the hillside in the cotton-white snow.
Winter is the best season of the year.

Tierney Powell (10)
Whitminster CE Primary School, Whitminster

Fish - Haiku

Swimming up and down,
bubbling in the blue ocean,
around and around.

Leanne Williams (9)
Whitminster CE Primary School, Whitminster

Ali Baba

I have a little pet tortoise
His name is Ali Baba
He is 6 months old
He does not like it in the cold.

He likes to walk very fast
But in a race
He will not come last.

He likes to eat a lot of food
If he does not get any he will go in a mood
He likes to keep very healthy
By eating and drinking.

He loves to sleep all day and night
But watch out, he might bite
He has a very hard and a big shell
And a very small head
Underneath rocks are his bed.

Nicolle Youngs (10)
Ysgol Iau Abergwaun, Fishguard

My Guinea Pig

I've got a guinea pig called Ziggy
Who eats lots of food like a piggy.
He's fat and he's round
He must weigh a few pound.

Cuddling Ziggy I like best,
He makes the hay look like a nest.
Cleaning the hutch out is the worst,
It looks like it's just going to burst.

He has a little friend called Fudge,
She's always giving him a nudge.
They like to play outside on the grass
While they look at the shiny, sparkling glass.

Danielle Davies (9)
Ysgol Iau Abergwaun, Fishguard

My Rabbits

I've got two lovely rabbits
who are coloured black and white,
they're very small and fluffy
and they sometimes give me a bite.

The white one is called Salt
and the black one is called Pepper,
they live in a hutch outside
where I serve them a big supper.

I clean the hutch every weekend,
I give them hay and straw,
they really like carrot and toast
which they eat with their *big paws!*

At Christmas I bought some leads
to take them for a walk
but because they are so different
they're like cheese and chalk!

Charlotte Harries (9)
Ysgol Iau Abergwaun, Fishguard

Dolphins

D olphins are big, dolphins are small, they come in all shapes
and sizes
O ver the waves they jump
L ively under the sea with its friends
P eople like to watch them swim and jump
H elp the dolphins, you can adopt them and make a difference
I n the sea they use echo location
N ice, juicy fish is what they like to eat
S o let them be free to swim in the sea.

Kirsten Jenkins (11)
Ysgol Iau Abergwaun, Fishguard

My Cats

Onw and Dids are my two cats,
With such big fluffy tummies.
They sit like couch potatoes
Looking at the telly
But when I come home
They come running to the door,
Following me wherever I go.
Sleeping outside my bedroom,
Sitting by the bath,
Trying to lap the water
As it comes out of the tap.
Miaowing at the window,
Waiting for their food.
Chasing birds and butterflies
And sometimes a weenie mouse.
I love my big, fat cats,
My mischievous tabby cats.
Hiding in the bushes,
Climbing up the trees,
Purring when I tickle
And rub against my feet.
My Onw and Dids
Are the best of all the cats.

Naomi Khan (9)
Ysgol Iau Abergwaun, Fishguard

Friends

F orever being kind to you.
R eady to help you at all times.
I s always honest with you.
E ntertains you when you're sad.
N ever lets you down.
D efends you in an argument.
S urprises you all the time.

Ruth Evans (10)
Ysgol Iau Abergwaun, Fishguard

A Poem About Money!

Money, money, money
Full of joy,
Come to me, I need a toy.
Money, money, money
Full of fun,
Is like my mum,
So give me some.
Money, money, money
My name is Roy,
I broke my toy
And I've got no joy
Without money, money, money
It's no fun.

Who cares? At least I've got my mum.

Adam Davies (9)
Ysgol Iau Abergwaun, Fishguard

My Grandpa

I love my grandpa
He's just so mad
He acts really silly
Like he's just a lad!

He loves to tease me
And tickle me too
I laugh so much
Sometimes I need to rush to the loo.

We have so much fun
Just talking and playing
He is my best mate
That's all that I'm saying.

Gareth Rhys Owen (7)
Ysgol Iau Abergwaun, Fishguard

The Haunted House

One night when the moon was shining bright,
Some children had a very big fright!
But what they saw was a very big owl
And they heard a great big howl.
What a racket, they thought
But all their ice creams they had bought.
They fell on the floor
Because there was writing on the wall!
Then it all went dark
And there was a great big spark.
Something's wrong, they feared,
Everything was acting weird!
Then there was a loud *bang!*
And the door went *slam!*
Something wriggled, something moved, is it a mouse?
Then a ghost appeared,
It's something bad, they feared.
They started to run
All the way back to their mum!

Esther Phillips (9)
Ysgol Iau Abergwaun, Fishguard

My Friend Scott

I have a friend called Scott
We always talk a lot
About our PlayStation games
To beat each other is our aim
We talk about Lord of the Rings
And lots of other things
I like him a lot
My friend Scott.

Rhys Tyrrell (9)
Ysgol Iau Abergwaun, Fishguard

The Four Seasons

Spring is when the flowers grow,
Daffodils stand all in a row.
Birds are cheeping,
Lambs are leaping,
Pink blossoms scatter when the winds blow.

Summer is when the skies are blue,
Trees are green, the grass is too.
Waves crashing,
Dolphins splashing,
Holidays for me and you.

Autumn is when the sunsets glow red,
The hedgehogs and dormice have all gone to bed.
The swifts have flown,
The swallows have gone,
All the leaves the trees have shed.

Winter is when the north winds blow,
Children are asking, 'Will it snow?'
Log fires glowing,
Outside it's snowing,
Santa is coming, ho, ho, ho.

Ruth Jenkins (11)
Ysgol Iau Abergwaun, Fishguard

Spooky

Werewolves make an awful howl
Whooos flying around the night sky
But a spooky owl.
The haunted house is very cold.
All the chairs are very old.
I wonder what will happen when you go there
But all I can say is *beware!*

Elen Rees (9)
Ysgol Iau Abergwaun, Fishguard

The Silver Fish

Sparkling as the
moonlight shines
down on the
calm, flat sea.

Like a shark
swimming
flicking its tail
like a hand on a clock
beneath the
calm, flat sea.

Flashes past the
clouds of seaweed
as quick as a bullet
as reflective as a mirror
darting about under
the calm, flat sea.

Rhianna Chilton (11)
Ysgol Iau Abergwaun, Fishguard

Back To The Good Old Days

Why do we text, e-mail and page?
Think of all the money we'd save!
Enough of the TTFN and the L8r,
Why not get back to good old pen and paper?

A letter is personal and straight from the heart,
Why and when did all this start?
Don't get me wrong, I do the above,
But as from today it'll be the personal touch.

Chloe Williams (10)
Ysgol Iau Abergwaun, Fishguard

My Gateway

I walked up a path,
I walked quite slow
Then suddenly I saw a glow.
I walked towards the glow,
It was my only light,
It was very bright, oh, what a sight!
As I opened the gate
I saw multicoloured hills
And then I got the chills.
I looked up and I saw a sun,
It was bright blue
And for some reason it looked like goo.
Then I knew it was time to go
And as I walked back the sun turned purple
And crossed in front of me was a turtle.

Philippa Jullien (11)
Ysgol Iau Abergwaun, Fishguard

The Rocket

The rocket went up in the sky
To see the stars and the moon.
It went up very fast
With a big, big blast -
And a noise that went *boom.*

The men and women saw lots of things
Like the Earth, it was as small as a ball.
When they came down they turned round and round,
Faster than ever before.

Natasha Lewis (11)
Ysgol Iau Abergwaun, Fishguard

Sunday Football

Every Sunday morning
my alarm goes off at eight
and twenty minutes later
I'm by the garden gate.

We meet up in the car park
and jump aboard the bus
which takes us down to Pembroke
all thirteen of us.

When we arrive at the venue
we're all raring to go
the referee blows her whistle
and we're standing toe to toe.

Our opponents are from Tenby
we drew with them last time
but today we're going to beat them
by seven, eight or nine.

I pass the ball to Charlotte
she passes back to me
I shoot for goal and hit the net
and we all jump with glee.

Charlotte scores a third goal
and Chloe adds another
as Hannah scores our fifth and sixth
she is cheered on by her brother.

As half-time fast approaches
and we are six-nil up
Hollie makes a great save
and we hope to win the cup.

The second half is now underway
and I increase our lead to seven
goals eight and nine do follow
we're now in seventh heaven.

The final whistle has sounded
and we have clinched the win
nine-nil, we're delighted
let the celebrations begin!

Sophie O'Connor (10)
Ysgol Iau Abergwaun, Fishguard

My Little Brother

Joseph is a busy boy
A singing bear is his best toy.
Every day he crashes and zooms
With Henry Hoover around the rooms.
Joseph runs around the house
Like a bomb.

When he's tired he'll watch Tractor Tom!
Cute blue eyes are what you see.
Our cuddles and hugs
Are special to me.

Abigail Dunn (10)
Ysgol Iau Abergwaun, Fishguard

The Storm At Night

Lying in my bed at night,
The noise it came, I had such a fright!
The wind was howling,
The rain was lashing,
My poor old window was getting a bashing.

The thunder roared, the lightning struck,
Our old oak tree fell into the muck.
The place to be, most definitely,
Is in my bed, comfortably.

Sam Phillips (10)
Ysgol Iau Abergwaun, Fishguard

I Love Sport

Every day I go and play,
When the sun is in the sky,
I go to golf, I have such fun,
I go with my friend and am driven by my mum.

We play football, it gets very tough,
To kick the ball and try not to be rough,
We score goals time after time
And I can hear my mum and my sister on the line.

Gymnastics I do to keep me fit,
I bend my legs and do the splits,
A medal we won just the other day,
When we came home my teacher said, 'Hooray!'

We do our best when our teacher puts us to the test.
We love our sport we do in school.
Football, golf, gymnastics
And swimming in the pool.

Chloe Sinnott (10)
Ysgol Iau Abergwaun, Fishguard

Meg

My dog Meg is black and white,
She's a Jack Russell terrier
Who likes to play day and night.
She likes to run through the fields,
Chasing rabbits if she can.
She's so full of energy
And I'm her number one fan!

Lauren Thomas (9)
Ysgol Iau Abergwaun, Fishguard

Plasticine

I like plasticine.
It starts off cold and hard.
I bash it and I mash it,
I pull it and I squish it
Until it no longer feels like lard!

I like plasticine.
I like to feel it in my hands.
I mould it, I shape it,
I bend it and I break it
From dinosaur to snake to orang-utan!

I like plasticine.
It gets stuck under my nails.
I squeeze it, I stretch it,
I squash it and I cut it.
I make it into slugs and snails!

Callum MacLeod (9)
Ysgol Iau Abergwaun, Fishguard

My Dad

I think my dad is funny
He calls me Princess Honey
He works hard all day
And takes me to the pool to play.

He goes to work wearing braces
And likes to watch car races
My dad has nice blue eyes
And likes to eat steak pies.

The best thing about my dad, you see
Is when he comes home from work to see me.

Isabel Dunn (8)
Ysgol Iau Abergwaun, Fishguard

Cubs

I go to Cubs on a Thursday
With my friends Michel, Sean and Rhys
We have so much fun
And we always get something done.

We cook, draw and play games
As Akela shouts our names
We play football, hockey, chess and draughts
With many other packs.

We try to earn badges in all that we do
I have thirteen but there are still many to do
At the end of our meetings we stand in a circle
Bow to the flag, pray and say
Goodnight, Cub Scouts, goodnight, Leaders.

Matthew Morgan (10)
Ysgol Iau Abergwaun, Fishguard

The Borrowers

T iny little people
H urry or we'll be seen
E ars listening to the tiny, scurrying feet.

B orrowing is what they do!
O h, where's my thimble gone?
R unning here
R unning there
O h, such busy, little people!
W hat would they do without their holes in their walls?
E ating chunks of cheese and slices of chocolate
R epeating every step of the way
S h, sh, because there they go again!

Jessica Tannahill (10)
Ysgol Iau Abergwaun, Fishguard

Weather Of The Week

On Monday till Tuesday
the weather was fine
but still I wonder
where's the windchime?
Did it blow to the east?
Did it blow to the west
in a big man's mouth?
Wednesday was the same
but with some clouds and some rain.
In the forest it was warm
in the town there was pain
but still it carried on, that terrible rain.
On Thursday it was different
funny feelings inside.
Butterflies twinkle, so does my mind.
My heart has reminded me that it is spring
birds and plants and the animal king
has come to sing.
Friday is miserable, everyone's sad
some people crazy, some people mad.
No butterflies, no birds, no animals, no herds
except for a single drop of rain
from the clouds above.
Saturday and Sunday were the funniest days
children and adults have the best games
with balls and toys, dolls and noise.
They played happily together forever and ever.

Angharad Portch (9)
Ysgol Iau Abergwaun, Fishguard

Dogs

Dogs are my favourite animals,
They're the ones I adore
But Boxers are my favourite breed
Or it might a Labrador.
Sometimes they get all grumpy,
I'd just leave them alone,
Try to cheer them up a bit,
Give them a chewy bone.
Then they get all sleepy
And now it's getting late,
Get them into bed
And wake them up at eight.

Lauren Bell (9)
Ysgol Iau Abergwaun, Fishguard

My Car

When I'm older I am going to buy a sports car.
It's going to be silver and shiny
And it will be very, very fast.
My car will have a roof that comes down
And big wheels to make it go fast.
There will be four leather seats inside
To take my friends for a ride.
I'm going to drive it all over the world
To lots of different countries.
London to see Big Ben,
Africa to see lions and giraffes and
Lapland to visit Saint Nicholas.

Liam Jones (8)
Ysgol Iau Abergwaun, Fishguard

The Night

The night was soot-black
As I walked home
The road was empty
As I walked alone.

The night called darkly
As I walked home
The owls hooted loudly
As I walked alone.

The night closed around me
As I walked home
The moon shone around me
And I no longer felt alone.

Michael Jenkins (11)
Ysgol Iau Abergwaun, Fishguard

Money

M oney is cool, you can buy lots of things
O ne thousand pounds
N inety pounds
E ven a million pounds
Y ou can enjoy your money.

There is lots of money in the world
Even on the floor
Just like my bike
I like to rally on my expensive bike
I like rallying down the streets and alleys
I would like to be rich.

Gemma Lawrence (11)
Ysgol Iau Abergwaun, Fishguard

The Wedding

I went to my mother's wedding
It was a lovely day.
Me and my sister were bridesmaids
When she got married in May.

Our dresses were colourful
A really nice blue.
My cousins Emily and Sophie
Were bridesmaids too.

So was my aunty Victoria
She had to come from away.
The wedding was in St Mary's
And then we went down the bay.

My mother married Stuart
Jerome was his best man.
Everyone had a lovely day
And I danced all night with my nan!

Hollie Owen (9)
Ysgol Iau Abergwaun, Fishguard

My Bike

My bike is a pro bike
It's shiny and blue
My bike is a mountain bike
And it's fun to ride too.

My bike is a fast bike
And I like to rally
My bike is a shiny bike
When it speeds past the alley.

Jack Ribbons (11)
Ysgol Iau Abergwaun, Fishguard

My Dog Smot

My dog Smot is a sheepdog
I love him lots and lots
He has a white coat covered with black spots.

He enjoys going for long walks
Out in the countryside, down to the beach
Playing with his ball
But 'Smot, fetch', we are unable to teach.

Digging holes in the garden is what he likes to do
Burying his bones deep in the ground
To keep them safe and sound.
His tail wags and his mouth grins
I think he loves us as much as we love him.

Ffion Williams (10)
Ysgol Iau Abergwaun, Fishguard

Ice Cream

I like to be seen
Eating ice cream
In front of people
I think are mean.
Although I am keen
To stay
Terribly lean
I cannot stop
Eating ice cream.

Thomas Kilmister (9)
Ysgol Iau Abergwaun, Fishguard

My School

Pens and papers,
Teachers' files,
Math books and math files,
Computers and chairs.

Mrs Watkins teaches science and technology,
Mrs Evans teaches history and music,
Mrs Evans gives us maths in the morning,
Mrs Watkins takes us swimming.

Alice and Ellie are my friends,
Alice has got short hair whilst Ellie's is long,
They are both good friends
And are good at football.

Mrs Williams and Mrs Jones
Give us a scrummy dinner,
Spaghetti and beans, chicken and turkey,
Ice cream, yoghurt, cheesecake and fruit.

All in all it's a very good school,
I think everyone in the world should come.

Rhiannon Moreton (9)
Ysgol Pennant, Penybontfawr

My Favourite Book

My favourite book
Is not called Hook
Because there is no such book!
My favourite book is not called Hairy
It's not even scary!
My favourite book is not so rare,
You can find it everywhere
And I know where!

My favourite book is the dictionary!

Jake Fox (9)
Ysgol Pennant, Penybontfawr

School Friends

Huw my friend just loves football,
He's in Year 4 and very tall.

Tomas Owain my good mate,
He's always in a right old state.

Tomas Evans he's very fast,
I'd never think that he'd come last.

No offence but Joe's quite small
And in rugby he likes to maul.

Rhiannon she is quite bossy
But sometimes she is quite fussy.

James Guilar is very big,
Sometimes he eats like a pig.

Our school teachers are very clean
But in class they can be mean.

Edmund Layland (9)
Ysgol Pennant, Penybontfawr

My Cat

My cat, what a waste of space!
Just coming into the kitchen
and there he would be
lying on my chair.

My cat, disgusting,
disgraceful cat,
licking himself,
his luxurious, shiny fur.

But what a cat!
A fantastic, furry friend!

Rhys Evans (10)
Ysgol Pennant, Penybontfawr

Today I Saw . . .

Today I saw a little worm
Wriggling on his belly,
Perhaps he'd like to come inside
And see what's on the telly!

Today I saw a little fly
Buzzing round the school,
He is a very sly guy
But sometimes is a fool!

Today I saw a little fish
Swimming in a pond,
He said that he had a wish
To meet the spy James Bond!

Emma Beech (11)
Ysgol Pennant, Penybontfawr

Animal Numbers

On my way to school today I saw . . .

10 terrible tigers
 9 nasty newts
 8 enormous elephants
 7 silly seals
 6 slimy snakes
 5 fat frogs
 4 fabulous flamingos
 3 tasty tarantulas
 2 trembling turtles
 1 orange octopus.

Jade Poole (10)
Ysgol Pennant, Penybontfawr

School

Our school has lots of books
and children have scornful looks.
Some children have excellent brains
and the spiders go down the drains.
We have mathematics which is boring
and spelling tests which are very rewarding.
I like school dinners
and playtimes too
but art is the best -
it beats all the rest!
School can be fun all day long
but home is where I belong.

Heidi Breeze (11)
Ysgol Pennant, Penybontfawr

If I Go To The Woods

If I go to the woods what do I see?
Three bears. I hope they haven't seen me!

If I go to the woods what can I find?
Three bears. I hope they're kind!

If I go to the woods what can I feel?
Three bears' claws. Are they made of steel?

If I go to the woods who can I hear?
Some snarling and *snap!* Was that my back?

If I go to the woods what can I find?
The guts of a bear. I've been gobbled up inside.
Goodbye!

Gus Harris (10)
Ysgol Pennant, Penybontfawr

My Friends!

I've got cousins, second cousins, friends, best friends,
so here they are.

My friend Ellie is quite tall
She has long hair that is sort of gold.

Marks out of ten for being a friend
I'd give ten out of ten.

My friend Rhiannon is very tall
But she doesn't like to play football,
In fact when I think about it
She's scared of the ball.

I suppose my brother's a friend
So I'll tell you about him.

My brother James is taller than me
Sometimes he wants to stomp on me.

I wish I could do the same to him
But I can't
But I suppose I'll live
Longer than him!

Alice Ashton (9)
Ysgol Pennant, Penybontfawr

Under My Bed

I think there's a monster
Under my bed,
When I'm asleep
It nibbles my head.

I think that the monster
Under my bed,
Tortured my teddy
And ripped off his head.

I don't think the monster
Under my bed,
Likes eating dust mites
Instead of my head.

I think that the monster
Under my bed,
That after he's eaten
He turns the brightest red!

I think that the monster
Under my bed,
Is a very naughty monster
For nibbling my head!

Bradley Merchant (11)
Ysgol Pennant, Penybontfawr

My Bedroom

Open up my wardrobe
and what do you see?
A pair of dusty slippers
and a broken TV.

Open up my drawer
and what do you see?
A little box of make-up,
a spare plaster for my knee.

Open up my school bag
and what do you see?
A half-eaten apple
and my homework (history).

Open up my toy box
and what do you see?
My moth-eaten teddy
and my bunny called Lee.

Open up my bedroom door
and what do you see?
A pair of angry eyes and
a mouth shouting, *'No entry!'*

Lowri Mai Jones (10)
Ysgol Pennant, Penybontfawr

The Cave

I was walking through a cave
and what did I see?
Four goggly eyes glaring down on me,
shall I go further or shall I go back?

I was walking through a cave
and what did I see?
Five lizards slithering beneath me,
shall I go further or shall I go back?

I was walking through a cave
and what did I see?
Six sneaky spies spying on me,
shall I go further or shall I go ba . . . *argh!*

Tristan Curteis (10)
Ysgol Pennant, Penybontfawr